Contemporary Artist Residencies
Reclaiming Time and Space

Taru Elfving,
Irmeli Kokko,
Pascal Gielen (eds.)

Antennae-Arts in Society
Valiz, Amsterdam

Contemporary Artist Residencies

Reclaiming Time and Space

Taru Elfving, Irmeli Kokko,
Pascal Gielen (eds.)

Contributors

Livia Alexander
Nathalie Anglès
Helmut Batista
Taru Elfving
Pascal Gielen
Francisco Guevara
Maria Hirvi-Ijäs
Jean-Baptiste Joly
Patricia Jozef
Irmeli Kokko
Donna Lynas
Antti Majava
Vytautas Michelkevičius
Nina Möntmann
Marita Muukkonen
Jenni Nurmenniemi
Bojana Panevska
Alan Quireyns
Florian Schneider
Ivor Stodolsky

Contents

Part 5: Transitions

Reclaiming Time and Space
Introduction

Taru Elfving &
Irmeli Kokko

Residencies for artists and curators have gained increasing significance within the ecosystem of contemporary art in recent years as crucial nodes in international circulation and career development, but also as invaluable infrastructures for critical thinking and artistic experimentation, cross-cultural collaboration, interdisciplinary knowledge production, and site-specific research. Meanwhile the ongoing processes of wider societal changes—economic and geopolitical pressures as well as the impact of ecological and humanitarian urgencies—are affecting the arts, professional practices, and mobility in ways that raise ever more urgent questions concerning sustainability and access.

The globalization process and the all-pervasive effects of the creative economy together with the increasing growth of the art market have all had an impact on the latest developments of artist residencies. However, the core function of residencies continues to be in support of artistic development, to provide time and space for art, research, and reflection. Residencies have today become attached not only to biennials, museums, scientific research centres, and universities, but also to urban regeneration projects and even airports, shopping centres or other businesses of various kinds. While residencies are further integrated into the intensified processes of production and competitive career building in the arts, concurrently new artist residency organizations are founded, often by artists, more as a breakaway from these structures.

The arising ethos behind the new residencies includes a search for more sustainable alternatives than the neoliberal condition allows for artistic practice. Now, the nomad artist[1] is characterized by diversity of possibilities, several alternative routes and roots in art and aesthetics, times and places—with an attitude of resistance against the standardizing forces of globalization. As international circulation has accelerated, residencies have remained points of critical encounters where local contexts can continue to challenge homogenization and its inbuilt power relations.

Against this background, the book *Contemporary Artist Residencies: Reclaiming Time and Space* asks: what is the present role of artist residencies in the contemporary art ecosystem? How do they meet the changing needs of individual artists? How can residencies provide alternative openings and infrastructures to nurture artistic work in the midst of current societal transformations and environmental crisis?

In order to address these questions, we have taken practice-based knowledge as the book's premise, while setting out to listen to the field and the residency practitioners themselves. The book builds on the discussions in the symposium 'Residencies Reflected',[2] on conversations with numerous residency organizations and residents, existing research on artist residencies, and our own professional experiences and insights working with and in residencies. We have chosen to focus exclusively on residencies within the field of visual arts, or specifically contemporary art, while recognizing the increasing fluidity of the boundaries between disciplines and the current development of residencies towards more multidisciplinary models. To begin with, our introduction lays the ground with a brief historical framework, based on Irmeli Kokko's research,[3] followed by an overview of key concerns emerging from the book.

A Brief History of Residencies

In the early nineties, artist residencies as a method and a formula seemed to correspond to many institutional utopias: creating art on site, experimentation, and artists' international mobility and interaction, all in the spirit of the famous Black Mountain College. Artist residencies made it possible to travel and work beyond the Western map of art, to new continents of art. In the residencies, different cultures met at a personal level. It seemed that this renaissance through residencies would be one of the best achievements of the globalization of art. Moreover, it also emerged in an unplanned fashion, like a grassroots movement without any guidance from governments.

Traditionally, artist residencies have been considered as places—as houses, communities of studios and apartments—where artists could retire to make art for a specific period. According to Maaretta Jaukkuri, the first head of the Nordic Arts Centre in Helsinki, in the eighties a lot of effort went into keeping exhibition operations and guest studio operations separate from each other. The traditional operating model for artist residencies, referred to as 'guest studio centres' in the Nordic countries, was based on the approach where the studio is a private work space providing the framework, time, and space for creating a work of art. The modern view regarded a work of art as an object that was independent of the location of exhibit and could be moved from place to place. A work of art was a nomadic item without a place, and the location of exhibiting a work of art was a pure and optimal space.

In 1992, the first, hefty phonebook-sized residency catalogue *Guide of Host Facilities for Artists on Short-term Stay in the World* was published in France. For the Guidebook a two-year survey was coordinated to identify and list venues for creative work with 'a new spirit'. Around 200 residency organizations from 29 countries and 5 networks were listed and included in the Guide. The selection criterion was based on the founding texts of a range of existing organizations that had adopted a certain ethos: to provide work space for research and experimentation and to encourage creative activities to create new contacts, either with other artists or with a specific environment. Openness and access to artists of all nationalities was also a fundamental criterion for the Guide. The contemporary residencies were seen to foster exchanges, encounters, and even confrontation. Residencies were seen as arenas in which the unpredicted could materialize, and as the studios to embody art in transition, not the gestation of the work itself.

Now, 26 years later, the Information Centre for Artists–TransArtists website provides information about more than 1,300 residency centres, the majority in the Northern hemisphere, in all possible geographical, institutional, and ex-stitutional contexts, and in between. Residencies today form a global sediment of flexible, semi-public, semi-private organizations and studios, where artists and art-professionals can travel, work, and live for periods of time in a variety of social, cultural, political, and economic circumstances in specific locations, climates, landscapes, and temporary communities with other artists and art-professionals.

There are different views regarding the recent history of artist residencies. According to Claire Doherty, the new wave of artist residency activity in the nineties was related to the combination of situated art practices and the tradition of artist residencies.[4] Miwon Kwon[5] expands this view with her argument on how the minimalism-related art conventions, which emerged in the sixties and seventies, changed how the nature of an art object was interpreted. Minimalism superseded the idea of locations having no meanings, and the idea of a work of art being independent of the meaning of the location. A new kind of connection was established between a work of art and the site of its making, and the connection could also require spectator presence. The idea of the connection between the site, creating a piece and exhibiting it formed the basis for different conventions of site-bound art, which are today referred to as site-determined, site-oriented, site-referenced, site-specific, site-responsive, site-related and project-based art. Since the nineties, art institutions have been increasingly interested in a site-bound approach as the starting point of creating works of art. This requires artists to be willing to travel and create art on site.

According to this view, the tradition of mobility and an international artists' communities, based on historical continuity, provided a readymade operating model in the nineties for the contemporary art conventions which required artists to travel and create art on site. Traditional artist residencies, artist centres and studio complexes were renovated to match the travel-oriented working methods of site-specific art practices, particularly in conjunction with biennials.

Also, in the twenty-first century, the creative workforce, such as exhibition curators at art institutions and elsewhere, started to come up with different curatorial strategies to provide support for artists creating art on site, especially in commissioning new artworks.[6] At the same time, artist residencies observed the needs of the field and adjusted their operating ideologies to match the connection between artwork and site. After that, studio work by an artist in residence took place within conditions affected by the location, its history, and the cultural/geographical or the socio-political environment. When in a residency, the artist works in a situation, not alone in a studio.

The success of residencies can also be explained by the active role they have in promoting the career development of artists in the global art market. According to Charlotte Bydler,[7] one of the effects of globalization was that people started to shun art exhibitions produced and distributed from the perspective of a nation state. Instead, artists, curators, and art dealers in the supranational network of the art sector move from one biennial and art fair to another. To have a successful career, art workers and artists have to be willing to travel. According to Bydler, since the late eighties, international residency programmes were specified so that they could offer a ready infrastructure for new travelling artists as they arrived at the heart of one art world after another. Bydler argues that from the perspective of international career building by Swedish artists, in the eighties extensive periods of working in artist residencies in the hearts of the art world were even more important than international exhibitions. The PS1 Contemporary Art Center International Studio Program, founded in 1976, managed a comprehensive international studio programme where artists from Australia, Sweden, China, Japan, Columbia, and Uruguay worked with support from different countries. According to Bydler, the artist list of New York's international PS1 Studio Program from the eighties onwards shows the decisive impact of international residency programmes on the career development of these artists.

At the beginning of the nineties, the governmental art departments started providing extensive support for the artist residencies in their own countries through studio programmes, which were significant in the international art sector. In the programmes, artists were also offered contacts to art dealers, curators, and international artist colleagues. In the spirit of the time, the residency organizations also started to network actively in the nineties. The international Res Artis network, founded in 1992, expanded rapidly and gained a growing membership. Res Artis annual meetings have taken place since 1993 as incubators for residency organizations, aimed at supporting the development of their practices.

Artists Nobility–A Pendulum Between Rural and Urban

In many cases, conventions in the arts are transformed by artists themselves, either as a reaction to existing conditions, or actively by means aimed at modifying the structures of art production. In fact, changes in residency operations can be considered in relation to their own tradition: artist communities. It is significant that artist communities expanded the notion of independent production towards collaborative processes of production as early as the late nineteenth century. The site of art production was regarded from the perspectives of the conditions, the location, environment, and community.

There is no consistent report available on the background and history of artist residencies. However, there are articles, lecture documents, and some art historical studies concerning the artist colonies of the nineteenth and twentieth centuries, and the avant-garde artist movements and artist communities. When outlining the evolution of residency operations step-by-step, there seems to be first a shift away from society, and then, as in the eighties, a shift back to the system. This pendulum motion involves changes and transitions, such as the industrial revolution and the world wars, during which the prevailing political and financial conditions either forced artists to go elsewhere, or artists voluntarily sought to form better intellectual and productive conditions for creating art, which often took place through artist communities.

Jean-Baptiste Joly, Director of Akademie Schloss Solitude, considers artist residency centres as gathering locations for artists similar to the sixteenth-century academies in Italy. The original mission and spirit of the academies was liberal–their task was to give artists freedom from professional guilds and the restrictions of craftsmanship. According to Joly, the Renaissance academy as a new forum for discussion, debate, and exchange of information can be equated with residency centres as distributors of innovation. European examples of those continuing this tradition include the Jan van Eyck Academie in Maastricht, the Rijksakademie in Amsterdam, and the Akademie Schloss Solitude in Stuttgart.

The international artist communities, artist houses and educational initiatives by artists in the nineteenth and twentieth centuries, in Western art history, are the predecessors of the existing, institutionalized artist residencies. There are many names for residency operations: 'künstlerhaus', 'artist communities', 'artist colonies', 'retreats', 'konstnärs gästateljee' and 'gästateljee centrum', each with its own history and geographical background.

Artist Colonies In the Nineteenth and Twentieth Centuries

In the United States in the eighteen-eighties, artists, authors, and scientists discovered the nature and native American culture of New Mexico–Taos and Santa Fe–which were on the verge of extinction. The artist colonies of Santa Fe and Taos represented communities created by the location and its culture, and the appeal of these communities encouraged artists of various art sectors–visual artists, writers and researchers–from many countries to travel there to investigate and document the disappearing way of life, religions, and art of the local pueblo Indians. All were impressed by 'the spirit of the place', as D.H. Lawrence expressed it. For example, the Finnish artist Akseli Gallen-Kallela worked in the colonies of Taos and Santa Fe for three years.

The MacDowell Colony was the first artist colony founded in an organized manner in the United States. Inspired by the American Academy in Rome, Italy, it was established in 1907 by composer Edward MacDowell and his wife Maria MacDowell on a farm in New Hampshire. Edward MacDowell had also founded the American Academy. After the death of her husband in 1908, Maria MacDowell had 32 artist studios built in the vicinity of the farm. The colony still has the same task: 'The Colony's mission today, as it was then, is to nurture the arts by offering creative individuals of the highest talent an inspiring environment in which to produce enduring works of the imagination.' Particularly in the United States and Australia, artist homes are a significant part of the continuity of residency operations from the twentieth century to this day.

In her book *Rural Artists' Colonies in Europe 1870-1910* Nina Lübbren writes about the scene of artists moving from cities to rural colonies in Central Europe from 1830-1914. A total of about 3,000 artists retired as a mass movement for different periods of time to establish artist communities in rural areas mainly in France, Central Germany, and the Netherlands but also in Hungary and the Baltic Sea region. Rural nostalgia as a counter reaction to urbanization and industrialization constituted the ideological framework for artist villages in the countryside.

The idea of creating new sensual experiences of nature was a central artistic agenda in the colony projects. The experience of giving oneself up to the countryside and being immersed in the sights, colours, sounds, smells, and details of nature led artists to develop their own brand of plein-air practice. New innovations, such as a studio moving on wheels and landscape painting methods, which preceded impressionism, were developed in the colonies. In paintings there appeared a new unfocused immediate foreground, the idea of which was to lead the gaze of viewers to the sensual experience of nature, to admiration and amazement.

The size of the colonies ranged from a few dozen to over five hundred artists. There were both international and national art villages. Artist mobility from colony to colony varied: there were artists who resided permanently in a colony, those who lived and worked in a colony for a specific period, and those who moved like nomads from one colony to another. When shifting from the early modern era to the modern era of urban bohemian artists in the early twentieth century, artist villages remained in place, but the rebellion involved in the role of bohemian artists no longer suited peaceful rural villages. After the First World War, artist colonies lost most of their significance from the perspective of art production, and the remaining villages became destinations for cultural tourism.[8]

From the Countryside Back to the Cities

Before the Second World War, European avant-garde utopian movements created cosmopolitan artist communities in the cities. Their programmes aimed to have an impact on the content of art, the relationship between art and society (life), art education, and the art institutions' operational methods.

In the twentieth century, the Blaue Reiter, De Stijl, Cubism, futuristic movements in Italy and Russia, Dadaism in Zurich, Surrealism in Paris, Russian avant-garde and Constructivism, as well as the Bauhaus in Weimar, created new aesthetic/political concepts, artist communities, art production methods and artworks. For example, the constructivism movement in Russia turned art into 'production art' and the artist into 'production artist' and studios into 'laboratories'. Walter Gropius founded the Bauhaus school as a counter reaction to the model of academic artist education, where the artist was isolated from society. Around Bauhaus he created an international artist community, workshops across different forms of art and practical/theoretical artist education.[9] During the first three decades of the twentieth century, cosmopolitan artist communities represented intellectual homes across nations, states, and language boundaries in a Europe of antisemitism, nationalism, restricted mobility and patriarchal power.[10]

As a result of the Second World War, many European artists and intellectuals fled across the Atlantic to New York. Modern avant-garde moved from Europe to the United States. New forms of educational and collaborative production emerged, such as in Black Mountain College (1933–1956) with its Summer Art Institute (1944–1956). During the summer residencies in the fifties visual artists, composers, authors and dancers of the American avant-garde, such as John Cage, Robert Rauschenberg, and Merce Cunningham, created the optimal model for an artist community and collaborative artistic work. The operations' focus was outside the institutional system, but they redefined the conventions and content of art; for example, creating methods for collaboration between different forms of art and context-specific working methods. The Happening was one of the achievements of the Black Mountain summer residencies.[11] The summer schools of Black

Mountain upgraded the idea of artist colonies as rural retreats into collective laboratories for experimental art. The PS1 residency centre in New York and the Künstlerhaus Bethanien in Berlin, both established in the eighties, represent the continuity of the avant-garde spirit of the Black Mountain College. Innovation now constituted the core of the activities of urban residencies. The goals of the urban artist residencies continued to promote the aim of analytic and historical avant-garde to redefine artistic conventions.

European artist communities of the twentieth century were socio-political and productive communities for art innovation. The ideological background of artist residencies in the twentieth century was first related to the industrial transition and its counter reaction, which was implemented as artists moving from cities to the countryside. Cosmopolitan artist communities of modernism and the avant-garde headed to the cities. The First World War created flows of artist refugees. The Second World War created a new flow of artist refugees, this time to New York. The PS1 centre was established there, as the first one representing new residency operations and setting an example for many future residency centres, such as the International Artists Studio Programme in Sweden.[12]

On the Run Once Again?

The increase in contemporary artist residencies is interconnected with the instrumentalization of art in the service of urban politics and the competition between cities from the eighties onwards. Creative economy hubs and their symbols such as museums, exhibition industry, and biennials are part of the same phenomena. Residencies have been at the heart of the globalization and mobility of artists, while they have remained at the margins of the international cultural industry. The paradoxical function of residencies has been to serve both as agents in the globalization of urban cultural politics and as local stations, where to 'land in a readymade infrastructure'.[13]

The space and time provided by residencies represent the same divided world as mobility (Zygmunt Bauman). Everything is conditional and depends on where one comes from. For the artists of the well-to-do North, residencies can be part of the international career service concept. Residencies in the metropolitan centres of the art world used to be highly desirable, but now they appear only meaningful if the service is good, outcomes are produced, and the residency can lead to contacts useful for career development.[14] Meanwhile modernity's promise of mobility, with its inspiration and poetics, as well as the nineties residency artist nomadism, has been replaced with the critique of ceaseless travel and deterritorialization at a time of digitalization and cheap flights.[15]

However, for the large part of the visual artists in the world, freedom of artistic work in their own homelands is impossible due to economic, cultural, and increasingly political reasons. The studio in a residency is for some artists a respite, a space that allows them to work in economic independence for a moment. A residency can then have significant importance for the development of the individual's artistic practice. Residency also provides an opportunity to reflect on one's practice to an extent that is not possible for everyone at home, where the field of art may be weakly developed or otherwise limited in scope.

Residencies are meanwhile increasingly integrating artists into various other sectors of society, from universities to technology companies, which are implementing artist residencies as instruments, usually aimed at dialogue. The practices and models of residencies are more and more turning outward, towards the world. Their focus is on cultural and societal development, rather than on that of the artists' careers. They are forging new connections and pathways between diverse regimes of society.

As in the case of ecological biodiversity, it is today necessary to resist the homogenization of intellectual, aesthetic, and cultural knowledge. This demands the creation of cosmopolitical spaces, where the navigation and negotiation of differences is possible. Moreover, this raises the question concerning the role of residencies in the process of cultural homogenization: are residencies reinforcing this, or are they supporting cultural diversity?

As we approach the twenty-twenties, the discursive shift is visible in the values of both residency artists and organizations. The impact of cultural homogenization is tangible in the homogeneity of urban living environments, following competitive city development, as well as in the commonality of art institutions with the art market. While the institutions, biennials, events, and buildings are growing in size, novel micro-organizations are proliferating as alternatives. What is the role of residencies in these transformations?

Residencies have been valued for their capacity to provide production services and networks in urban environments, yet now opportunities for further education, reflection, and focus are in high demand. Independent margins, geographical and other, have gained new interest. Small size can be a qualitative criterion. Difference and diversity are valued. The Microresidence Network, an international network of local residency programmes, is one example of this phenomena. It resembles a molecular structure, based on specificities rather than on standardized services in urban contexts.

The 'new spirit' of the twenty-twenties requires better acknowledgement of modes of interaction between local cultural traditions and Western contemporary art. While there are reasons to embrace the critical debate concerning residencies, it is worth reminding of the potential of residencies. Residencies hold their own history, value, and function in relation to artistic communities. They nurture artistic work and its development, create connections and spaces across cultural differences, and support the opening of local contexts. In the *Policy Handbook on Artists' Residencies*, the evolution of residency practices since the nineties has been described as a process of re-assessment where the interest on 'how' has shifted to the question of 'what' is done. It is now time to also ask 'why'.

In These Times and Spaces

'The Great Acceleration is best understood through immersion in many small and situated rhythms. Big stories take their form from seemingly minor contingencies, asymmetrical encounters, and moments of indeterminacy.'[16]

It can be argued that what characterizes the present is the intensification of disjunctions (of time and space) distinct from the linear time of the progress narrative in modernity and the flat networked space of postmodernity.[17] Viewed from the perspective of Northern Europe, where we are currently editing the book at hand, this appears as a time of rupture—of enforced migrations, reinforced borders, regressive patriarchal politics, growing economic inequality, return of fascism, unpredictable extreme weather phenomena, escalating extinctions, and much more. The past and the future clash in the present, while here and elsewhere no longer have clear coordinates.

Therefore, as the international art world appears to be accelerating in its global circulation at a dizzying pace, it is worth pausing to question: who are affected by this acceleration and how? Where does the circulation take place? Artist residencies are certainly an integral part of the machinery, yet at the same time their paradoxical role is to counter this very acceleration as support structures for artistic development, offering space-time for creative processes and momentary retreats for critical reflection. Their role is thus to recognize and nurture diverse temporalities rather than succumb to the productivist ethos of homogeneous linear time. Or, they can make time for 'the relations between a diversity of coexisting temporalities that inhabit interdependent ecologies'.[18]

The starting point of *Contemporary Artist Residencies* was to explore the role of residencies as particularly focused on reclaiming time and space for creative experimentation and critical reflection freed from, even if momentarily, the accelerating pressures of production. However, the valuable open-ended time-space offered by residencies for artistic work is not uncorrupted by a neoliberal logic articulating every space and time in economic terms, as a potential place to make profit and scarce time to be capitalized on. The ambition of this book is to offer a critical analysis of the changing role of residencies, but also to present emergent strategies and methodologies that can be seen to reclaim time and space.

Reclaiming should be understood in this context, and in relation to the residency models discussed, not as a return. Rather it has to do with active envisioning, sensing and making sense, and imagining into being. Moreover, it is crucial to avoid universalization as 'one never reclaims in general'.[19] What the time and space to be reclaimed is, and how this may happen in residencies and by diverse practitioners, depends on myriad variables. This book does not claim to offer a broad overview or generalizable conclusions, yet it does present a plurality of situated practices and reclaiming operations that connect with and at times also contradict each other, across a number of points.

Heterogeneity of time and space requires a heterogeneous set of approaches. And the field of artist residencies for sure is incredibly diverse and constantly evolving. Due to this multiplicity it is especially crucial that the residencies critically situate themselves, as a report by Res Artis, the international umbrella organization for artist residencies, argues in terms of evaluation.[20] Residencies serve the needs of artists in different ways, at various stages of their careers and artistic development, not only in response to different kinds of practices but also in significantly different contexts. The terminology and emerging discourse on residencies, alongside modes of assessment, have to remain faithful to this complexity. Otherwise they lose touch on the core function of residencies, which is to follow creative processes without predefined routes or goals, unafraid of risks.

This function does not sit comfortably with the increased pressures to measure impacts and outcomes. A number of articles point to the challenges faced today in navigating this minefield. Both the definitions and assessments of residencies are particularly problematic when driven by external forces and interests, often in stark contradiction to the values and goals of residencies themselves to foster open-ended experimentation and reflection. Yet, the writers also emphasize the necessity to acknowledge the shifting parameters of artistic practices and the changing needs of artists, which demand that the organizations' goals and modes of operation are evaluated and rethought accordingly.

The critical question that emerges out of many contributions has to do with how residencies can respond to the effects that societal transformations have on the art ecosystem and artistic work. This requires critical awareness and articulation of the aims and means of the organizations, which form the base for regular re-evaluation rather than external measures. Yet again, this mission is integrally connected to the support they give artists and to their particular role in the field, which are neither disconnected from, for example, political tendencies and ecological urgencies.

On Collectivity

While residencies are more and more attentive to their role within the wider ecosystem of the arts, they are also entangled in complex ways in the growing pressures on financially precarious artists and curators. Residencies are integral in the international network and career development, which is characterized by the so-called 'residency hopping'–a particular stage in professional development that borders on a nomadic life style and impacts both artistic discourse and practices in numerous ways. The other side of the coin reveals that residencies are not simply a privilege, and not always a retreat, but also a significant part of contemporary survival strategies in the arts–offering short-term grants, studios and accommodation.

It can therefore be questioned, whether residencies in the end reinforce individualism, in line with much of the art world structures and economy built on individual careers and names. Could they be in fact isolating practitioners while aiming to bring them together? They are surely, in part, also feeding competition—from one open call to the next—even when encouraging sharing and critical reflection. Residencies may well present a potential for alternative, more sustainable economies of self-organization, but what does it take to nurture collectivity within the structures that allow and encourage us to be mobile in the present? Moreover, what is the impact, value, and potential of travel beyond network and career opportunities—for example, in terms of transformative encounters across disciplinary, cultural, and geographical boundaries? Or, how is this default model for an international career built on residency circulation implicated in the economy of the arts more widely?

The book poses the above questions but cannot claim to provide definitive answers to them. The contributions do, however, acknowledge the dilemmas —of access, precarity, sustainability—haunting residencies, while actively developing practical responses to them. In diverse ways, the residencies discussed here are reclaiming self-directed, open-ended space and time for artistic work. Yet they also challenge the traditional ideas of artistic autonomy by directing attention to the complex processes that the work of artists is entangled in, from specific cultural contexts and geopolitical frameworks to material conditions, power relations, and privileges. Autonomy can only take place under certain conditions.

What arises out of the articles is a shared emphasis on the significance of conversations and collectivity. Peer-to-peer structures are integral support for artistic practices and their development, and in residencies their role appears manifold as they form the ground for both critical dialogue and professional networks. How residencies can nurture these temporary communities, and the emergent relationships built on trust and generosity rather than on competition or exchange, remains a key concern to the field. Furthermore, the relation between the momentary communities in residencies and their surrounding communities (local, artistic, multispecies, and more) raises ever more urgent questions.

On Connectivity

There appears to be no escape in this age of omnipotent 'action at a distance', whether understood in terms of online networks or unequally distributed effects of climate change. Residencies find themselves today, therefore, located at the intersections of the unsettled dichotomies of private and public, home and elsewhere, temporary and permanent.

Residencies are removed to an extent from not only the everyday of the artists' practices, communities, and contexts, but also from their usual art world structures and discourses, hierarchies and histories. Meanwhile, residencies remain connected through various flows. First of all, work for elsewhere, deadlines and new opportunities follow artists around the globe. Residencies are also plugged into the intensified international art world circulation of today that has led to its discourse and community to be always simultaneously everywhere and nowhere. Residency programmes, furthermore, often focus on mediating professional dialogue and public engagement with the local scene and audiences in diverse ways.

Art and artists today are identified as a key instrument in urban development and community planning. Meanwhile, artistic work can take place anywhere today, seemingly even in constant mobility. Space-time experiences and the role of residencies are affected by digitalization so that the borders between, for example, centres and peripheries have become less certain. The articles, however, challenge the illusion of a smooth networked space in a number of ways. Drawing attention to the specificities of the residency contexts, they demand and foster sensitivity to the complex histories and ongoing processes of change—colonial and ecological, amongst others—in each site and situation. Digitalization is part and parcel of these interwoven transformations and urgently calls for further in-depth examination that is beyond the scope of this book.

Furthermore, the complex coordinates of mobility are currently being redrawn by ecological, political, and economic crises worldwide. Reinforced borders, enforced migrations, and climate change raise acute questions concerning sustainability and unequal access also in relation to artist residencies. The articles touch upon these challenges and present some strategies that residencies are developing in response to them. Yet this book can only offer a starting point in this urgently needed critical thinking and radical experimentation in the face of the uncertain future.

Notes

1 See e.g. the description of 'altermodern' artist: Bourriaud 2009.
2 The Residencies Reflected symposium was co-organized by Academy of Fine Arts/University of the Arts Helsinki, Frame Contemporary Art Finland and HIAP Helsinki International Artist Programme in Helsinki, November 2016.
3 Irmeli Kokko, *Taiteilijaresidenssien rooli nykytaiteen tuotannossa*. Jyväskylä: University of Jyväskylä, 2008. http://urn.fi/URN:NBN:fi:jyu-200807015572.
4 Claire Doherty, 'The New Situationists', in Doherty 2004, pp. 1-13.
5 Kwon 2004, pp. 1-19.
6 Doherty 2004, p. 46.
7 Ibid., pp. 50-55.
8 Lübbren 2001, pp. 1-4.
9 Harrison and Wood 1992, pp. 221, 339-340.
10 Charles Harrison and Paul Wood, 'The Individual and the Social', in Harrison and Wood 1992, p. 549.
11 Goldberg 1984, p. 54.
12 Bydler 2004, p. 50.
13 Ibid.
14 The artist Mikkel Carl, in the presentation session of 'artists experiences'. Res Artis Conference, Copenhagen, 2017.
15 See e.g. Steyerl and Buden 2006.
16 Tsing et al. 2017, p. G5.
17 See e.g. Malm 2017.
18 Puig de las Bellacasa 2015.
19 Stengers 2018, pp. 140-141.
20 See research led by Mario A. Caro as Chair of Res Artis network, published e.g. in Gardner 2013.

Literature

— Bauman, Zygmunt. *Globalization: The Human Consequences*. Cambridge, MA: Polity Press, 1998.
— Bourriaud, Nicolas, ed. *Altermodern: Tate Triennial 2009*. London: Tate Publishing, 2009.
— Bydler, Charlotte. *The Global Art World INC: On the Globalization of Contemporary Art* (Acta Universitatis Upsaliensis. Figura Nova Series, 32). Stockholm: Almqvist & Wiksell, 2004.
— Doherty, Claire, ed. *Contemporary Art: From Studio to Situation*. London: Black Dog Publishing, 2004.
— Gardner, Sarah, ed. 'International Perspectives on Artist Residencies.' *D'Art Topics in Arts Policy* no. 45 (2013).
— Goldberg, Roselee. 'Performance, a Hidden History.' In *The Art of Performance: A Critical Anthology*, edited by Gregory Batticock and Robert Nickas, pp. 24-36. New York: E.P. Dutton, 1984.
— *Guide of Host Facilities for Artists on Short-term Stay in the World*. Paris: L'Association Française d'Action Artistique (AFAA), 1992.
— Harrison, Charles, and Paul Wood, eds. *Art in Theory 1900-1990: An Anthology of Changing Ideas*. Oxford: Blackwell, 1992.
— Joly, Jean-Baptiste. *About the Necessity of Residential Centers in the Contemporary Context of Art*. www.resartis.org/en/activities__projects/meetings/general_meetings/1996_-_dublin/jean-baptiste_joly/.
— Kaplan, Caren. *Questions of Travel: Postmodern Discourses of Displacement*. London: Duke University Press, 2000.
— Kwon, Miwon. *One Place after Another: Site-specific Art and Locational Identity*. London: MIT Press, 2004.
— Lübbren, Nina. *Rural Artists' Colonies in Europe 1870-1910*. Manchester: Manchester University Press, 2001.
— Malm, Andreas. *The Progress of This Storm: Nature and Society in a Warming World*. London: Verso, 2017.
— OMC Working Group on Artist' Residencies. *Policy Handbook on Artists' Residencies: European Agenda for Culture: Workplan for Culture 2011-2014*. S.l., 2014. http://ec.europa.eu/assets/eac/culture/policy/cultural-creative-industries/documents/artists-residencies_en.pdf
— Puig de la Bellacasa, Maria. "Making Time for Soil: Technoscientific Futurity and the Pace of Care." *Social Studies of Science* vol. 45, no. 5 (2015), pp. 691-716.
— Stengers, Isabelle. *Another Science is Possible: A Manifesto for Slow Science*. Cambridge, MA: Polity Press, 2018.
— Steyerl, Hito, and Boris Buden. 'The Artist as Res(iden)t'. *Etcetera* 24, no. 104 (December 2006), pp. 29-32.
— Tsing, Anna et al., eds. *Arts of Living on a Damaged Planet: Ghosts and Monsters of the Anthropocene*. Minneapolis: University of Minnesota Press, 2017.

Part 1

Residents and Residencies

The Temporary Resident, a Sequel...

Alan Quireyns

A residency is not a journey. It is not casual. I am facing the challenge of living my life somewhere else for a couple of months. My work is the constant. It survives all places, each new experience. It changes, but it always builds on what is already there. The exchange with the foreign environment, new people, and myself lends an edge to my work. I gain new insights, I see other possibilities and I unravel knots that for a long time I had felt could not be disentangled. A friend once said to me that whenever he had to take an important decision he went somewhere he had never been before. Then, upon his return, he knew what to do. A residency may look like an escape but it is much more of a confrontation.

My head is always lagging a bit. During the first days I stubbornly hold onto the things I brought with me from home. Mundane objects obtain a new glow. Before putting my feet into my slippers, I pick them up. I turn them around and see where the relief has been worn out by my heels. The sole is thinner there too. In my thoughts I list the places where the slippers have taken me. The soles of my feet relax when they recognize the familiar profile. With the swiftness of a magic trick my new place of residence becomes recognizable. Only now do I dare to move about here. I walk around, shift a table, a chair, the lamp on the bedside table. Adapting means work.

Change breaks habits, as if they have to make room for new ones. I look for this situation. It makes me very receptive to impressions. My senses reach out like antennae. They feel, smell, and taste. I dwell in a labyrinth of streets I've never walked before. Time and time again I get lost, as I refuse to take the same route twice. My body registers the city. After a few days, certain routes emerge and I notice how new habits establish themselves. Before long they may change into routines.

Each place is unique. I know this but nonetheless I have to suppress the urge to compare. Nobody likes to hear that their situation is similar to others. That's why I listen. I collect the stories of the people I meet. I embody a paradox: the stranger who arrives today and stays tomorrow. I am not just passing through. People find it reassuring that I will stay for a while but that one day I will leave again. They provide me with stories and opinions, and even unburden themselves sometimes. They change my ideas, crush preconceived notions, sharpen perspectives. They ease me away from the person who I was.

Time is solidarity. I take the time to get to know a situation from the inside. To quietly look at all its aspects. I take the time to be a witness, a sponge, a fly on the wall, hearing and seeing everything. Sometimes the others take up my time unsolicited. I don't mind, quite the contrary, but I also like to remain in control. Because I like *giving* my time to somebody. I look people up, I talk, I hang about, apparently aimless but always alert. Taking one's time consciously also slows down the time of others. People like it when you say that you have time. I practice time.

When I'm listening, I remain silent. I am aware of my privileged position. I can travel anywhere without having to think about my origins. And yet I can't help drawing parallels now and then. The attacks restore the balance between the continents in a morbid way. Old borders are given new life. Soldiers have been patrolling the streets for so long now that they have become invisible. They are now part of the grey façades of my hometown. I'm not looking for a contest about which country is in worse shape. Sometimes, reality is too real and people need a utopia. I too need a utopia. Like the town hall I found here. On the ground floor double wooden doors lead to an auditorium. With the new building an open-air theatre was created at the back, with stands made of stone. As I entered the hall, I heard children laughing. There was a school theatre competition going on. This town hall employs a sound and light technician, and festivals, and theatre and singing competitions are held here, introducing culture right at the heart of society.

Every morning I buy fresh bread at the baker's. At first, he was surly, almost rude even. A tourist, I saw him thinking, who will be gone again tomorrow. But when I appeared for the fourth time he made an effort to chat, with the five words of English that he knows. His reserve is now gone. Each day he is a little bit more curious. I am waiting for the question of what I'm actually doing here, and for how long.

I am the stranger who arrives today and stays tomorrow. I answer questions posed to me, but not all of them. My origins are not important. When I say where I come from I am treated to pity or I see the twinkling in the eye of the person I'm talking with. What's it like to grow up there? Now I have become someone that can be shaped from the here and now. I try to stay formless as long as I can, just as I postpone adopting new habits as long as possible. Here, people don't know where I grew up. Whether I am rich or poor. Here, the only thing that counts is what I'm doing now. I see this as a form of deliberate statelessness. In the residency I can evoke illusions. Of not having any relatives, no brothers or sisters, mother or father. That there is an indeterminate force, which has driven me to this place. And that that same force will one day take me somewhere else. I do not enter into long-term relationships. My main goal is to live in between everything. Between worker and intellectual. Between activist and lazy bum. Involved *and* anti-social. I try to unite as many contradictions as I can in myself.

I base my wanderings on self-made sketches. The busiest traffic arteries form the spine of my map. This map is a negative: the places I know best are least indicated on it. They are blind spots as I can find my way there with my eyes closed. Sometimes my plan says 'watch out!', with an exclamation mark. Those are places where the air is thicker and I become aware of every slowing movement. Actually, I shouldn't mark them, as my body immediately feels I mustn't stay there. The rhythm of my steps is somewhere between purposeful and purposeless. It becomes more difficult to remain committed to something. I have gotten used to the luxury of following no one but myself. A thought comes into my head and before I know it, I am executing it. Doing rather than thinking.

Every once in a while, I meet someone. I make an effort to open up. I decide not to wear sunglasses even though the sun hurts my eyes. When my gaze crosses that of someone else I do not avert it. My path changes. Instead of living in evasive curves I step right up to people, nod to them, talk to them. I look for quiet cafés where I can work on my drawings without being disturbed. Before long, however, someone will look over my shoulder, asking me where I'm from, wishing me welcome. Sometimes I make a drawing of them, but mostly of fictional characters in the form of a cartoon. They function as a diary. Such a character experiences the same things that I experience. I make him dream and long for things that I long for myself. One of the men to whom I show my drawings introduces himself as Huertas. He talks to me about his work: minuscule booklets that he leaves everywhere in the city, in open spaces, windowsills, and footpaths. They are his gifts to incidental passers-by, so they can read them. He cuts out the five-centimetre pages himself and staples them together. One of these booklets is made from an old school atlas. Each page is a fragment of a world map with figures on it and letters composed of small red bars of equal length. He explains to me that the length of such a red bar is equal to that of the Berlin Wall. He lets the wall travel, places it in China, Mexico. It is shocking how much space the wall occupies. He gives me a copy to take home with me. So far, he has made about twenty of them.

There are other artists in the residency too. I am not alone. They have all found their own ways of communicating with the city, to create their work in response to the lack of direct communication, to having to adapt to different habits and different rules. Ella asked people to take her to a place in the city that they find special. There they pick out a spot where Ella then paints a tiny piece black, with Chinese ink. Sometimes in plain sight, but just as well under a rock or a loosened tile. Despite the fact that the action takes place in public space it is an intimate, shared moment between Ella and her guide. In all, she does so eight times. She enjoys the thought that the black spots will remain and that her guides will still sometimes go there. I think that with this action Ella has created a memory that will live on long after the black has faded. With her work she finds a way to communicate beyond language.

Patterns begin to emerge in my observations. I frequently see the same clothes pop up and the same people doing exercises in the park. A fountain tries to spout its water high up, as steadily as possible. Its effort is inspiring as on the grass of the water's edge a man is looking at the fountain, sitting in lotus position. A few days later there's four of them. I look for groups of people and how they move through the streets. I watch their behaviour, their choreography, how they try to stay together. How the roles are divided. Or elderly men staring at a construction site, with concentration, their hands on their backs. Constructions are sights in any city. They provide an opportunity to look inside, to get to know the construction, and the bigger the site the more euphoric its progress.

The most suspicious people are people like me, roaming the streets alone and in silence. Watching, taking notes and photographs and taking this material back home, as if conducting anthropological research. As if I'm not really a human being but someone on the outside studying the behaviour of mankind. I fantasize about where my subjects will go later. I imagine the houses where they come from.

Dark clouds are gathering, I notice, on the top deck of the bus. The bus drives on, relentlessly. It doesn't look like I'll be getting back soon. 'I've left my raincoat', I realize with a start. Then my panic reaction dissolves into a smile. Now I will have to come back.

This text is composed of fragments of conversations with the visual artists Saddie Choua, Ella De Burca, Koba De Meutter, Breyner Huertas, Ria Pacquée, Ryan Siegan-Smith, Amir Farsijani and Babak Afrassiabi in residencies in Mexico City, Ramallah, Teheran, Cali, Antwerp and other cities, organized by AIR Antwerpen and assembled by Alan Quireyns.

Time and Space to Create and to Be Human

A Brief Chronotope of Residencies

Pascal Gielen

> It is time to review human beings as the beings who result from repetition. Just as the 19th-century stood cognitively under the sign of production in the 20th under that of reflexivity, the future should present itself under the sign of the exercise.
> Peter Sloterdijk, 2009

> You have to play... It is especially important to try out things without observing yourself. You have to forget yourself while you are creating.
> Patricia Jozef, 2017

From Studio to Residency

This is how it starts. Three men enter the auditorium, clumsily carrying an incredibly large pipe. The thing is so gigantic that it has to be lifted over part of the audience, not without risk. These gentlemen seem to be amateur movers. You know, like the friends who help you haul a wardrobe up the stairs when you move house. They all know the best way to do it and each of them thinks his advice is better than that of the others. Doing things with a lot of fuss—mucking about. However, in the performance *Atelier* (Studio)—a coproduction of the Belgian and Dutch theatre companies STAN, Maatschappij Discordia, and Co. de KOE—all this is done without words. For a hundred minutes, one botched-up action follows another without the actors exchanging a single word. We are after all in an artist's studio, that sheltered space of highest concentration, focus, quiet, contemplation, and being intimate with oneself. Here, the artist has all the time of the world for himself and especially for his work. Here, the artist is completely in control, still experiencing the romantic illusion of artistic autonomy at its best. Studio time is therefore personal 'own-time' and studio space the 'own-space'. Here, it is the artist who decides how much time to take or to waste. In the studio artists can still be completely lost in time as they simply forget to look at the clock. In the space of the studio anything still goes because no-one is watching. And if by chance someone is, it is usually a close friend or an intimate partner. It makes the studio the perfect place for *doing*, for trial and error, just as in the early years of everyone's life. So, no words are uttered in the studio, at most some incomprehensible muttering and mumbling, alternated by an exuberantly joyful cry as something finally seems to be working out. All the things artists do in the studio, everything they can and may do, is therefore completely different from what is publicly told and written about those same artists. In Patricia Jozef's novel *Glorie* (p. 164) one of the protagonists, the artist Bodine Bourdeaud'hui, has this to say:

> After a number of interviews, I wondered whether I was the only one who knew that the best work originates in moments when I am not thinking about what I'm doing. At the moment where I let something happen.
>
> People often think that good art is the product of good thinking, whereas the daily practice in the studio is of a completely different nature.

The studio is the space par excellence of amateurish messing about, endless ambition, grotesque self-overrating, immense irritation, and always recurring self-doubt. It is the cradle of every creation and therefore of the unique experience of being human. In any case, the feeling that we are capable of creating something new is one of the fundamental characteristics of the human condition, according to philosopher Hannah Arendt (Arendt 1958/2018).

It is little surprise then that most artist residencies try to emulate this setting. Many residencies see it as their first noble task to stimulate and optimize the creative process. It is no coincidence that quite a number of places offered to artists for a temporary stay are located 'in the middle of nowhere'. In nature, on an island, or at least in the countryside, far from all urban confusion and the professional art world. The hosts of such residencies understand only too well that they must leave the artist alone as much as possible. The space for tinkering they are offering is after all immensely valuable in arriving at a brilliant work of art. Still, no matter how meticulously simulated, an artist residence is not an artist's studio. No matter how little the host tries to interfere with the artist, no matter how much it is stressed that no concrete results, let alone a finished product is expected, still the resident does not fully have the same experience as in his or her own studio. It is the experience of time and of space that marks the difference between a residence and a studio, precisely because both are institutionalized here in a different way. The own-time of the studio is replaced by the socially determined time of the host organization. After all, residencies do not last forever. The artist is given a month, three months, sometimes a year, or, in exceptional cases, five years to freewheel, but in all cases the duration of the residency is limited in time. Even when an artist rents a studio and knows that he can only stay there for a while, then still the mental horizon is different: if there is any deadline at all, it is the artist who imposes it upon himself. In the residency, by contrast, the deadline is imposed by someone else. Whether it is for a month or five years, the host organization determines when it ends. And even more: although no concrete results are required, the host organization does expect the artists to make their stay a meaningful one. This means, in the first place, that they are expected to be artists and therefore to do what artists do: create things. No matter how immaterial or unfinished these creations may turn out to be, the host does expect the artists to spend the allotted time in an artistic way. Of course they are allowed to mess about, it goes with the territory, but all these 'trials' should demonstrate some meaning or direction, a direction that always points to a potentially artistic result. Again, unlike in the studio, it is not the artist who expects this meaningfulness, but someone else—someone who is usually not their partner or intimate relation but rather a professional or at least an art aficionado. Whether it is an open call, a personal invitation, or an advanced selection process, the time and expectations are determined by others. The same seems to apply to the use of the space. The artists are of course expected to leave the space in neat condition when they go home again, but during their stay they are expected to leave traces of some artistic thought processes, even if only virtual or on a laptop. After all, the space was 'liberated' for creation. And again, this also goes for the artist's own studio, but here it is again someone else who does the liberating. And even though social control may be minimal, the artist knows to expect the question at any time: 'How did it go today?' or 'Any progress this week?' These enquiries do not regard the artist's health or mental state, but most definitely the artistic practice. Was there inspiration—as that is what the unique space and surroundings of the residency are for—or were any ideas developed, as that is what the allotted time is for. Yet again, this also applies to the studio, but in the case of an artist residency it is someone else who determines and sometimes even enforces this. In a residency, the own-time and own-space of the studio are transformed into a social time and a socially determined space. This also means that the artist-in-residence is subjected to a form of social control that carries both positive and negative social sanctions; things that artists decide for themselves within the confines of their own studio.

Residencies: a Chronotope

Somewhere halfway the *Atelier* performance the following happens. One of the actors extinguishes the lightbulbs hanging over the scene by submerging them in a pot of black paint. It is dark now. Is it inspiration that has gone? It may be any artist's biggest fear: the moment of not knowing what to make anymore. This experience may range from a small crisis to a burnout or even to big existential questions. Creation is after all the raison d'être of every artistic soul. To quote Arendt once more: to create is a fundamental experience of the human condition. Perhaps this is why many artists are tempted to leave their studios when experiencing a crisis. In any case, the longing for a different environment and a time that is different from the daily routine often originates in the hope of inspiration. This is true for still young and searching artists who have not (yet) fully seen the light but also for mid-career artists hoping to find new sources elsewhere. Even very successful artists can feel it coming–the moment they see they are only repeating themselves, become stuck in the rut of their own ideas. Then it is high time for an escape, a getaway.

Scanning the self-descriptions of residencies on the Internet and other media one can't help but notice how they play into this artistic hope. Almost all AIRs 'sell' themselves as places of inspiration. Whether urban or rural, they all advertise something appealing that will light or rekindle the fire in the residing artist in question. However, although just about all residencies make this claim, they do this in fundamentally different ways. They are rather varied in their ideas about how and where an artist may find inspiration. Time and space can again be noted as a distinguishing principle. After all, this is what residencies have to offer: the time and space to create. How they provide time and space differs greatly. This makes both notions convenient coordinates to arrive at a typology. Or, more accurately, a chronotope. The residency does indeed provide time and space for creating, but it also makes time and space mesh in a certain way. The notion of chronotope was introduced by Michail Bakhtin in 1973. With this neologism the Russian literary scientist expressed his view that time and space are symmetrical and absolutely interdependent. In any case, since modernity they make up the observation grid by which modern man understands himself, places himself in the world and organizes his labour and therefore also his cultural production. As to the latter, Bakhtin focused mainly on literature, particularly on the novella, in order to better understand both the production and perception of this artistic genre (cf. Gielen 2004). Here we will use the notion to look at and order the world of residencies. Let it be clear right from the start that we are talking about a Weberian typology, i.e. an idealtypical one (Weber 1904). This means that in reality we will rarely encounter the residencies as they are presented here in a pure form. Also, different AIRs are characterized by a mix of the following types. An ideal type serves mainly to sharpen our analytical observation. The empirical reality usually turns out to be much more complex, nuanced, and gradual in nature.

My Chronotope

A first chronotope was in fact already described above. Many residencies attempt to simulate the time and space conditions of the artist studio. Preferably far from civilization or at least from the art world they generate the time and space for the artist to engage in introspection. Away from the routine and from day-to-day worries the resident is given the opportunity to concentrate in isolation. The most extreme forms of isolation are to be found in residencies such as the one in Dry Tortugas National Park in Florida, or Outlandia in Glen Nevis (Scotland). The latter is situated at the foot of the UK's highest mountain, perhaps not by coincidence. Like the hermit, the artist hopes to see the light here through ascesis and introspection. The difference is that this light does not appear in a transcendental sky; the artist has only his profane self to rely on for dragging his creation from his own innermost depths. Sometimes there is beautiful nature, which helps, but it is mainly through existential acrobatics that the resident hopes to reach creative heights. The isolated place is supposed to generate the endless time for digging deep into himself, even though this time is limited to the duration of the residency. This type of residency is grounded in the belief that creation has to come from our deepest self and that talent is something one is born with. Isolation then only serves as what philosopher Peter Sloterdijk calls 'anthropotechnics' (Sloterdijk 2009). It is applied here to wrestle a brilliant idea from oneself in Buddhist concentration. Creation is indeed like a child that must be delivered. And as all mothers know, this requires hard and most painful labour. And it is especially me, myself, I who has to do the work.

Although the view of the artist as an unworldly genius may be a bit obsolete, it seems that the number of residencies in the countryside, on an island, or in grand nature is on the rise again. The motives behind this renewed exodus towards lonely mountaintops may today reside less in a belief in the own genius, but rather in an overdose of stimuli generated by a hectic art world in the grip of the creative industry and creative cities. In such a context, artists have to be social creatures and they have to network if they want to be successful (Gielen 2014). Creative hubs, collective incubators, and co-creative policies require social behaviour. And even if the artists hide in their studios, the World Wide Web and social media vie for their attention. Isolation is becoming an increasingly scarce good, but one that is quite essential to doing creative work. After all, to create is to concentrate. But since the eighties, the so-called professionalization of the art world calls for a different type of artist. Faith in the individual genius gradually made way for a rather soberer look on artistic activities. After the slovenly dressed artist of the sixties and seventies came the artist in tailor-made suits, meeting with equally well-dressed gallery owners, art collectors, and more or less independent curators. Talent alone simply doesn't sell, after all. The artists themselves will have to go the extra mile by exploiting their cultural credit through social capital. Cultural sociologists like Pierre Bourdieu (1977) did well by that in those days, with their analyses in which they grounded art and artistic talent primarily in a collective belief. The brilliant artwork simply originates in a *social* alchemy. In a word, in the eighties artists were obliged to have both feet firmly on the ground. Talent as such is no guarantee for a successful career. The artist dressed in black who thinks that behaving like an 'anti-social' figure in some corner is cool, is gradually becoming obsolete in the eighties. The Mondrian-like type mumbling to himself makes way for socially clever guys like Julian Schnabel. This professional reset also required a different model of residency, with a quite different chronotope.

Network Chronotope

It was perhaps no coincidence that it was a sociologist who put the Amsterdam Rijksakademie [the Dutch National Art Academy] on the world map. From 1982 onwards, Janwillem Schrofer implemented an open studio policy there to keep subsidizing governments and sponsors happy. Although there are still artists with their individual studios, the international beau monde of the art scene that comes by every year draws most of the attention. The Academy becomes the place to be, a hub in a network where every artist looking for success must have resided for a while. The emphasis is still on the highly individual development of the residents, but not without having a chance of being discovered. If you want to build a career, you must be visible to talent scouts and the Academy played into that in the eighties. Just like PS1 in New York, this residential setting is no longer at the edge of the world but right in the urban centre where the nerve paths of art and capital cross. This network residency still cultivates the ideal of the idiosyncratic talent but seamlessly links this to the professionally required social activity. The residing artist not only has the benefit of very professional and high-quality artistic advice but is also provided with an artistic steppingstone. Those who don't make it after a stay at the Rijksakademie have only themselves and their limited talents to blame. Anyway, a network residency provides plenty of social opportunities. The chronotope here looks completely different from that of the residencies 'out there'. The situation is not characterized by introspection but rather by exhibitionism. It is after all not just about seeing but just as much about being seen. A place in the city that is well-connected to the art world increases the chance of being 'picked up'. This also defines how time is experienced. It is a feeling that is defined in particular by the highly networked place: the time pressure that is measured by the space one needs for jumping off. This has to happen within the timeframe of the residency. Whereas in the My Chronotope stress results from the fear of not finding enough creativity in one's innermost self within the allotted time, in the Network Chronotope stress comes from the fear that others may not discover this creativity in the artist in time.

Alter-Chronotope

Although discussions and debates in the Network Chronotope can be of a very high level in terms of content, they always revolve around creations and attempts by the individual artist. Her or his work is both the reason for a discussion and the potential of being 'picked up' and 'networked'. This is quite different in a residency where artists go for reasons of content. Whether it is about scientific, ecological, social/political or purely formal artistic/workmanship subjects, if a residency bases its selection of artists on either of these, yet another completely different chronotope is evoked. Even though building a career may be on the back of the artists' mind, time and space are primarily defined by content. Both the artist who travels to Antarctica to spend a few months in the company of scientists and the one who wishes to master ceramics at Keramis in the Belgian town of Mons, or the artist who enrols in a social practice residency: their motivation lies not in quickly gaining access to a professional network. The primary motive to engage in such 'thematic' residencies perhaps lies in the hope of further development, of better creation, and equally so of finding inspiration. These artists do not expect to find this inspiration within themselves, as in the My Chronotope, but notably outside themselves, in scientific knowledge, in a social issue, or in a convenient skill. Here the artists can lose themselves again in time and space but this time not through introspection but through exploration. They literally look for inspiration outside themselves. Time here is swallowed up by an interest in and fascination for a thing, a skill, a natural or cultural phenomenon. And space is there precisely because it brings this alterity, this otherness or the other in proximity. In other words, space here is defined by the proximity of something else and time by the relation to that other, for example the time one needs to master a certain skill, gain a scientific insight, or build a contact with a certain social group—hence Alter-Chronotope.

Although the appeal of such residencies is most certainly based on intrinsic motivation and sincere interest, their success can however also be explained in an alternative way. The current neoliberal climate, which sees art and creativity primarily in economic terms, creates a bigger demand for on the one hand virtuoso skills and craftsmanship and on the other hand for solutions to social problems (such as integration, and social cohesion). Both artists and residencies that focus on technical development or on community art are therefore favourably positioned when it comes to obtaining subsidies or sponsoring.

Embedded Chronotope

Whereas in the Alter-residency the chronotope is still defined by the time and space needed to understand the other or the otherness, the next chronotope suspends all time limits. Here the inspiration that is found is permanently invested in the space provided by the residency and goes way beyond the artistic domain.

While the aforementioned residencies or chronotopes in the end always served to invest in the artistic career of the artist, this last one completely opens up this investment to the rest of the world. Organizations such as the *land* foundation in Thailand tend to do this. Here, the time allotted to a resident depends on the time they need to get inspiration, realize a project, or simply restore themselves. So, this may vary from a few weeks to a lifetime. And the things an artist perhaps leaves behind have only their own transience as a time limit. Besides, they are embedded or, if you like, 'invested' in the space or the rice paddy, which is also used by farmers and other local people. Or, as it says on the organization's website: 'There is not a time limitation to the cultivation of the land, it is there to be used and can be used.' Resident artists have meanwhile constructed a gardener's home, a kitchen, and a bridge that can be used by both artist and locals. Residency here hardly serves to build an artistic career, but it does provide a way to be fully immersed in a society and its natural surroundings. Here, art coincides with life itself, or at least with life as some artist would have it. Residencies like the *land* foundation not only give central stage to the probing artist but to exercising mankind as a whole (cf. Schafaff 2018). Or rather, this exercise is regarded as the main occupation that accompanies life: trying, from the beginning to the end, to be embedded in a world. Here, the residency becomes a life's work with a chronotope that spans the entire duration of someone's life and where space covers no less than the entire planet in which a person tries to integrate. Such artists may never arrive at a finished artistic product, but consider their entire body of work as one big exercise in living. Such an exercise may go at least two ways: it either fits within an exodus, a permanent flight from the world whereby the artist only goal is self-development and mental satisfaction. Art then becomes primarily a therapeutic session of 'lifelong learning' and 'working on yourself'. Or, if this attitude orients itself to the world and the environment, it may also work as 'pre-figurative politics' (Boggs 1977), encouraging others to really experiment with a different life.

In any case, roughly speaking we can say in line with Sloterdijk (2009) that the nineteenth-century art world focused on the painting or sculpture, on the artistic product. In the twentieth century, this artistic product was defined by (self-)reflection and the discursive framing of the work. Perhaps the twenty-first century is open to the permanently practising artist. The artist as the lifelong resident of the whole wide world.

Towards the end of the performance *Atelier* the following happens. The three actors, rather pathetically, stage a crucifixion. It looks anything but devote, as in, for example, a painting by Jacob Cornelisz. van Oostsanen. The subsequent deposition of the cross is more reminiscent of that by Peter Paul Rubens, only then much more clumsily. Even dying is botched up in *Atelier.* Life is to keep on trying–until the bitter end.

Literature

— Arendt, Hannah. *The Human Condition.* Chicago: University of Chicago Press, 1958/2018.
— Bakhtin, Mikhail M. *The Dialogic Imagination.* Austin: University of Texas Press, 1981.
— Boggs, Carl. 'Revolutionary Process, Political Strategy, and the Dilemma of Power.' *Theory & Society* 4, no. 3 (Fall 1977), pp. 359-93.
— Bourdieu, Pierre. 'La production de la croyance: Contribution à une économie des biens symboliques.' *Actes de la recherche en sciences sociales* 13 (1977), pp. 3-43.
— Gielen, Pascal. 'Museumchronotopics: On the Representation of the Past in Museums.' *Museum & Society* 2, no. 3 (2004), pp. 147-60.
–. *Creativity and Other Fundamentalisms.* Amsterdam: Mondriaan, 2014.
— Jozef, Patricia. *Glorie.* Amsterdam: De Geus, 2017.
— Schafaff, Jörn. 'Building Bridges: Art as a Space for Rehearsal.' In *Commonism: A New Aesthetics of the Real*, edited by Nico Dockx and Pascal Gielen, pp. 345-61. Amsterdam: Valiz, 2018.
— Sloterdijk, Peter. *Je moet je leven veranderen: Over antropotechniek.* Amsterdam: Boom, 2009.
— Weber, Max. 'Objectivity in Social Science and Social Policy.' In *The Methodology of the Social Sciences*, edited and translated by Edward A. Shils and Henry A. Finch, pp. 355-418. New York: Free Press, 1904/1949.

From Community Building to Digital Presence

Bojana Panevska

The residency world is full of polarities: from institutionalized residencies to non-traditional spaces, from rural isolation to places that focus on production and organizing big-scale exhibitions, from community-oriented to finding solutions to particular socio-economic problems, and so on. Over the last ten years there has been a tremendous growth in residencies, not only in the Western world, but also in South and Central America, Africa, the Middle East, South/South-East/East Asia. This diversifying has brought many cross-over collaborations, and now, in 2018, it becomes obvious that we are still experimenting with the term and format of what a residency may be. A parallel can be drawn with the term Temporary Autonomous Zone (TAZ) being 'a temporary but actual location in time and a temporary but actual location in space' as Hakim Bey writes in his 1990 essay.[1] While the definition from the OMC working group in *The Policy Handbook on Artists' Residencies* (European commission 2015) is as follows: 'Artists' residencies provide artists and other creative professionals with time, space and resources to work, individually or collectively, on areas of their practice that reward heightened reflection or focus.'[2]

TransArtists,[3] the international platform on artist-in-residence programmes managed by DutchCulture,[4] centre for international cooperation, has the largest database of artist residencies, with the current number at 1526. To be part of the TransArtists database, residency organizers need to submit an online form and meet a number of criteria such as offering a residency opportunity that is not only a one-time opportunity; to be a professional opportunity (no B&Bs, resorts, and so on) and not aiming to make a profit from the residency programme; to be reasonably priced (if artists are expected to pay a fee); to accept international artists, and many other criteria. Furthermore, only programmes that provide accommodation or where the hosts provide concrete help in finding accommodation facilities are included in the database. Therefore, studio-only opportunities are rarely listed.

In 2017 there were 213 submissions for new residencies to be added to the database. From that number, 87 residencies were included, while for 2016 there were 189 submissions, from which 94 new residencies were included. Practically each year half of the submissions do not meet the criteria: they do offer time and space, but they lean more towards the experience of renting a room, without any other support or the experience of being hosted. Quite often the fee artists have to pay is very high, while they are not getting much in return.

In order to avoid abuse of the term 'artist-in-residence', there is a big challenge ahead of us in recognizing quality and professionalism and separating them from all the experimental models that are on offer. In this text I will distinguish four different approaches of residencies that are not only changing the format of the term, but also in their approach of working and of developing a project.

Helping Artists at Risk

In his book *Arts under Pressure* Joost Smiers writes:

> Although it has been claimed that we are all global citizens unhindered by social convention or contextualization, we are beginning to learn again that this is only partly true, while for most people it is not true at all. We also know that it is not desirable to be completely detached from our social surroundings. After the experience of delocalization that neoliberalism has offered us, we know even better than before that the world is too big and too complex for us to be able to orient ourselves within it and try to find something like a safe haven. This is a difficult subject, because we know for sure that many places on earth are not safe at all. There is no reason to romanticize the neighbourhood, the village or the fatherland. At the same time, it is true that refugees are not fleeing to 'the world' but trying to find a refuge in a particular, more humanely organized society.[5]

In these times, when (Western) countries' borders are opened only selectively depending on specific socio-economic criteria, it is of utter importance to have places where also artists can be safe (and sheltered) to express themselves. In many countries, state and non-state actors are increasingly restricting the work by and with critical artists as well as civil-society actors. Socio-political commitment in these countries results in personal danger to those involved. Therefore, the Martin Roth-Initiative[5] started as a joint project by the ifa (Institut für Auslandsbeziehungen) and the Goethe Institut in reaction to the global decline in pre-political spaces. The Martin Roth-Initiative promotes and supports endangered artists in close collaboration with a network of both national and international (cultural) institutions.

An example of a residency that is active in this field is Perpetuum Mobile (PM) in Finland. It has been organizing residencies for many years, hosting 'artists at risk' under various titles since at least 2013.[7] Another example is Artist at Risk Connection (ARC)—a global hub aimed at assisting imperilled artists and fortifying the field of organizations that support them.[8] ARC is a collaborative project led by PEN America and they are committed to improving access to resources for artists at risk, enhancing connections among supporters of artistic freedom, and raising awareness about artistic freedom.

At the other end of the spectrum, there recently was an open call for RESIDENZPFLICHT (RESIDENCE REQUIREMENT)—an artist-in-residence programme organized by the artists' group msk7 in Berlin.[9] The programme's goal is to use a diverse spectrum of artistic positions to temporarily open up the self-contained refugee shelters to approaches and developments in contemporary art. The RESIDENZPFLICHT art project will award ten project scholarships for one-month residences in the ten newly constructed refugee accommodations in Berlin between 2019 and 2020. The artists are invited to live for one month on the site of one of Berlin's Modular Refugee Accommodation Centres and create context-based artistic work there.

This last example shows how artists are creatively approaching the organizing of a residency with a strong focus on marginalized communities. This model of self- or artist-organized residency is widely popular, but especially in the non-Western world.

Self-organized Residencies

It is widely accepted that artist colonies are the predecessor of residencies, with the romantic idea of the artist to be in nature, secluded and having the time to focus on their work in peace and isolation. With cities becoming more and more expensive and weirdly gentrified, there is a tendency for residencies to move into rural areas.

More and more artists are taking matters in their own hands by organizing residencies. In some way they are establishing new models for residencies by experimenting with space, time, and funding. Very often this is done in a rural area, for obvious reasons of being more affordable, but also of reconnecting oneself with a different surrounding. As Mother Tessa Bielecki says in an interview:

> We feel this is an essential part of the desert experience. One needs to withdraw from time to time into these pristine wilderness experiences in order to be fully human. Everyone needs a touch of physical wildness in order to come really alive.[10]

Apart of inspiration, another crucial element of these residencies is revival of rural areas. I will use here as an example the Tsarino Foundation, which organizes artist-run artist-in-residency programmes in Tsarino.[11] It was set up in 2009 by an international collective of eight artists based in Amsterdam.

Tsarino is a small village in the Bulgarian Rhodope Mountains, near the Greek border. It was abandoned over thirty years ago due to a number of factors, one of which is its isolated setting amongst hills and forests. The foundation currently uses seven habitable houses, which have been renovated at a very basic level to provide artists with accommodation and studio space. Because the village is so remote and has no electricity, the conditions remain very basic. Through organizing residency programmes, the foundation wants to offer a platform for cultural exchange between the local community and (international) guest artists, as well as preserve Tsarino as a village.

Apart of helping (or creating) a community in a direct way, as the above example shows, there are also many residencies that work on the intersection of science and technology and in that way have a huge impact on society as a whole.

Art, Science and Technology

One of the pioneer residencies in the field of art and science is artists-in-labs in Switzerland. Since 2003, the artists-in-labs programme has been facilitating artistic research by way of long-term residencies for artists in scientific laboratories and research institutes. This programme is part of the Institute for Cultural Studies in the Arts (ICS) at the Zurich University of the Arts (ZHdK) and promotes sustainable collaboration between artists and scientists of all disciplines, not just in Switzerland but all around the world.[12] These long-term interdisciplinary and cross-border collaborations provide artists with an opportunity to critically engage with the sciences and their experimental and aesthetic dimensions. This includes explorations of the site of the laboratory, as well as a range of scientific topics, methods and technologies. As Harriet Hawkins writes:

> One of the things that became clear during our study was how many of the art-science projects either came explicitly or implicitly to challenge the institutional, scientific and artistic contexts and frameworks within which they were produced. At times such challenges were the raison d'être for the project and drove its forms of enquiry and mechanisms of practice. More often however, such challenges emerged through the very presence of the artist, through the questions asked, the daily practices undertaken and the work produced. Oftentimes these challenges, as discussed above, saw the knowledge making practices of scientists, their technologies, experimental procedures and their own ways of knowing reshaped and transformed. What we saw perhaps rarely, although importantly, was the reworking of institutional practice as a result of these projects.[13]

While in Eyebeam,[14] located in Brooklyn, NY, the works that are produced are ranging from the first-ever open-source social sharing tool (reBlog 2004) to more recently the open-source educational startup littleBits (2009), alongside arts activism such as the first Feminist Wikipedia Edit-a-thon (2013). In an interview I did with Laura Welzenbach, who was residency director in Eyebeam in 2016, she was talking about the social importance some artworks can have:

> One of our current impact residents is a great example. Tahir Hemphill joined Eyebeam as a resident a few years ago, and he worked on a rap lyric database. This became one of his tools to create content for his artwork. He came back to Eyebeam with the idea to use this rap almanac to teach youth. The Eyebeam education department immediately recognized the potential for this. It clearly can become an accessible way to teach kids a skill set around creative coding, reading and analyzing big data, critical thinking and so much more. We then started a trial session here at Eyebeam as an after-school program. In this case

> social impact, criticality, media criticism, and rap are tools to convey these contents.[15]

Seeing that more and more artists are working on projects with the aim of finding solutions to particular socio-economic problems, it seems only natural that residencies are embracing this need for cross-disciplinary collaborations.

Digital Residencies

In these times of great ecological and social pressure to find solutions for mobility, some residency organizers are experimenting with online residencies. To come back to the comparison with the term TAZ from Hakim Bey:

> The TAZ must also have 'location' *in the Web*, and this location is of a different sort, not actual but virtual, not immediate but instantaneous. The Web not only provides logistical support for the TAZ, it also helps to bring it into being; crudely speaking one might say that the TAZ 'exists' in information-space as well as in the 'real world'.[16]

Schlosspost is an English-language online platform for a global audience of young artists and those interested in the arts. Part of the Digital Solitude programme, the website was founded in 2015 by the international artist residence Akademie Schloss Solitude. The Digital Solitude programme provides fellowships for artists, designers, and web-based media researchers and offers online web residencies.

Web residencies' focus is not in the finished art piece; artists are rather invited to experiment with digital technologies and new art forms within a defined thematic framework. They're in direct exchange with the professional network of both institutions as well as a broad digital public which in turn gets immediate access to the artists' works. This format allows a decentralized and international discussion on topics set by the invited curators from the worlds of digital arts, net culture, and digital technology and society.[17]

In his text *The Praise of Laziness* (1993) Mladen Stilinović writes: 'There is no art without laziness.' And the organizers of the RFAOH residency interpret this in a very interesting way, by organizing the Residency For Artists On Hiatus (RFAOH).[18] This is a virtual yet functioning residency available to artists who, for one reason or other, are not currently making or presenting art. The residency exists in the form of a website only, and the residents are selected based on their proposals of 'on-hiatus' activities (or non-activities) through international open calls. All the projects are archived on the website with artists' activities such as having a permaculture farm; learning about brewing ingredients, procedures, equipment; long distance running, and so on.

Conclusion

With the constant renewal of old and tested ideas, different forms of hospitality are explored, and best practices are rapidly being implemented in different contexts and translated from local to global ones. Residencies do not exist in a bubble from the rest of the (art) world–rather, artists and organizers are actively rethinking their role in the community and society. This is especially true for the self-organized residencies that are prevalent all around the world, while the other models discussed in this text are primarily to be found in the Western world. This is not surprising, since a good (cultural) infrastructure and support is needed to organize these kinds of residencies, which many countries do not yet have.

There is a big challenge ahead in trying to support these initiatives and help them grow, while at the same time keeping the professionalism on a high level for both the organizers and practitioners. As the discussed examples show, the tendency to experiment on both sides is still growing stronger and has brought about changes in the institutions, and often in the surrounding communities and society as well.

Notes

1 https://theanarchistlibrary.org/library/hakim-bey-t-a-z-the-temporary-autonomous-zone-ontological-anarchy-poetic-terrorism.
2 http://ec.europa.eu/assets/eac/culture/policy/cultural-creative-industries/documents/artists-residencies_en.pdf.
3 www.transartists.org/.
4 https://dutchculture.nl/en.
5 Joost Smiers, *Arts under Pressure: Promoting Cultural Diversity in the Age of Globalisation* (Chicago: Zed Books Ltd., 2003), p. 82.
6 https://www.martin-roth-initiative.de/en.
7 https://artistsatrisk.org/about/?lang=en.
8 https://artistsatriskconnection.org/about-arc.
9 http://residenzpflicht.berlin/en/.
10 *Art Meets Science and Spirituality in a Changing Economy*. This book is also a catalogue of a five-day panel programme at the Stedelijk Museum Amsterdam (The Hague: Sdu publishers, 1990), p. 209.
11 www.tsarino.org/.
12 www.artistsinlabs.ch/en/.
13 Irène Hediger and Jill Scott, eds., *Artists-in-Labs: Recomposing Art and Science* (Berlin and Boston: De Gruyter, 2016), p. 53.
14 www.eyebeam.org/.
15 www.transartists.org/sites/default/files/station2station/2/.
16 https://theanarchistlibrary.org/library/hakim-bey-t-a-z-the-temporary-autonomous-zone-ontological-anarchy-poetic-terrorism.
17 https://schloss-post.com/about/.
18 https://residencyforartistsonhiatus.org/.

Part 2

Reframing and Intensifying Practices

Artistic Intelligence and Foreign Agency
A Proposal to Rethink Residency in Relation to Artistic Research

Florian Schneider

> It is not a spiritual renewal as fascists proclaim,
> that is desirable: technical innovations are suggested.
> Walter Benjamin[1]

1

In Latin 'to reside' means to remain. Turning back to the original notion of the term is particularly helpful when it comes to rethinking the very idea of residency. It connects space and time through a subjectivity that is based on and generates a somehow paradoxical effect: a continuity of temporary presence; furthermore, it is supposed to generate outcomes that sustain, no matter how they perform; and in doing so, it prepares the ground for the possibility to affect change.

Recapitulating such a general understanding of residence is the starting point to revisit both, artist-in-residence projects as well as newly emerging research residencies—regardless of the formal or informal character of their commissioning context. Deploying both approaches in a hybrid, rather than concurrent fashion, enables a notion of the artistic research residency as an interplay of artistic research and production with a specific understanding of their spatial and temporal conditions. This allows to speculate on their impact on three levels: as a format, as a concept, and as a potentiality.

As a format, residencies have become increasingly relevant in today's art world. In contemporary art, the past decades were characterized by programmatic turns that widened its outreach on a theoretical and increased its ephemerality on a practical basis. It triggered an intensifying pressure on individual artists to perform and sustain a meaningful existence. This pressure is multiplied by an increased level of competitiveness due to, among other reasons, an extensive growth in the number of highly educated artists all over the world.

As a consequence, residencies have responded to the pragmatic necessities of managing the precarious existence of artists. In addition to all their specific purposes and disconnected contexts, they provide a space-time that operates at the very limit of the creative act; they allow participants to escape the existential pressure, to reframe, intensify, or refresh their own practice. It is important to recognize that this aspect of the residency triggered a rather unspectacular revival of the format in both traditional institutional and non-institutional or newly emerging 'ek-stitutional'[2] environments. There are numerous and very different approaches to understand the residency today as a line of flight out of the mundanities and everyday occurrences of the art world. Examples range from the artist-run Performing Arts Forum PAF near Paris, or the artist-in-residency projects in the squatted cultural centre Macao in Milano, to the commissioned artistic in situ research project 'CAVEAT!!!', initiated by the Brussels-based artist group Jubilee.

It is thanks to both, the institutionally aligned and non-aligned initiatives, that the format of the artistic research residency might turn out today as a leverage that could also enable a radical rethinking of the role of art in society. In a sense that a residency never emerges for its own sake, but connects various different spaces of creative production, it proposes an understanding of innovation in artistic research that is no longer constituted by the disruptive character of the new, but by its capacity to reinvent connections between disconnected spaces across different layers of time.

Concept

This could be the main reason why, secondly, as a concept, various forms of artistic research residencies are proliferating across different sectors of society. Over the past years, private corporations, large institutions, universities, local municipalities, small and medium size enterprises have begun to create a wave of new residency programmes for artists. From the London Zoo to container ship residencies, from airports to scientific laboratories such as CERN in Geneva, they seem to share only the terminology with the original concept of offering artists a retreat from society to focus on their creative production.

Rather than at a remote distance, far away from the influences of a general economy and its unavoidable obligations and distractions, artistic research residencies are nowadays embedded in the middle of knowledge production. They can be found in any branch of creative of cognitive industries, given the circumstance that these indsutries are slowly becoming aware of their own, critical state. Residency projects such as Platform 12, a joint venture between the Robert Bosch GmbH corporation, Akademie Schloss Solitude, and the artist-run project Wimmelforschung, are designed as spaces for critical reflection. Remoteness is replaced by a criticality that is 'irrespective of the organizational structure of the company or the day-to-day work in the office and laboratory'.[3]

Potentiality

Here, rethinking the residency as artistic research enters a third level: as a potentiality, the artist in residence is questioning the inherent understanding and common preconceptions about the economies of knowledge production. The more or less explicit goal is to reveal its critical state and therefore enable a sort of 'capitalist self-criticism' that creates the conditions for change and innovation. Rather than staying apart from the arenas that are economically relevant, artists are both committed and commissioned to observe, participate, and intervene in the processes of value creation in cognitive labour and immaterial production, from small start-ups to large industrial scales.

Of course, being economically invested in affective and cognitive processes of production is nothing new for artists. Since the Renaissance, a modern understanding of art has generated a wide range of various flavours of a role model in which artists conceive of themselves as entrepreneurs of a self. It operated within specific, self-sufficient economies that generate affects as well as forms of insight and knowledge based on the power of being affected. But today, art serves a different purpose: it is supposed to play a crucial, and most importantly, a rather functional role in an economy that realizes excessive forms of value in terms of pleasure, entertainment, hope and care.

The generic expertise of artists has become increasingly valuable in fields of technology where innovation is no longer understood as the constant optimization of a process, but as its radical rethinking and remaking. The frame narrative of design thinking driven by 'rapid conceptual prototyping'[4] assigns artists a very special role due to their capacity 'to think outside the box' which is considered a prerequisite for creating innovations.[5] In return, the experimental setting is supposed to allow the artist to reflect a self that operates within such a system rather than from an alleged position outside of relations of production that strictly separate artistic and scientific forms of knowledge.

2

On April 27 in 1934, Walter Benjamin completed writing a speech that he was supposed to give at the Institute for the Study of Fascism in Paris, although he probably never delivered it. The meanwhile seminal text, published after his death under the title 'The Author as Producer' has turned into a source for constant inspiration, but its main argument is buried under mounds of selective interpretations serving different purposes.

In his fierce polemic Benjamin opposes the two most popular artistic positions of political engagement of his time: 'Activism' on the one hand and 'New Objectivity' on the other. He says that rather than asking, 'what is the attitude of a work *to* the relations of production of its time?' he would like to ask: 'What is its position *in* them?'[6]

In fact, Benjamin's proposal to shift from an attitude that is directed towards the relations of production to a self-critical investigation of the role of art as an immanent part of them, seems today more urgent than ever. One could even argue that the subsumption of public funding for the arts under the paradigm of the creative industries–often misunderstood as a 'neoliberal' strategy rather than as a key concept of social democratic cultural politics since the nineties–produces precisely the urgency to rethink the idea of residency. But this is done neither by lamenting and complaining about worsening conditions, nor by insisting on entitlements from a past that is long gone. According to Benjamin, it would require an attitude that challenges the presupposed authenticity and autonomy of art, while transforming the apparatus of production rather than just transmitting it.

Instead of conceiving the residency as a privileged position from where to look at the relations of productions, the artistic research residency could be re-examined as a relationship of production in itself and for itself.

The hypothesis is that the residency produces a peculiar kind of knowledge that reflects the position and the role of the artist as a 'foreign agency': an agency that acts for forces that are alien to the environment. Rather than observing, affirming, participating, or even immersing into it, the agency of artistic research sets out to make a local context feel and look strange. The further the research progresses, the less familiar it becomes with its own conditions.

Rather than balancing out, equalizing and standardizing the inconsistencies and incoherencies of a research process by establishing a seamless continuity of thought and its execution, the foreign agency of artistic research follows a different and experimental methodology. It operates through breaks and ruptures, standstills and sudden movements. Its aim is to engender a continuity of artistic practice within a discontinuous space of research, which is constituted by jump-cuts, rough confrontations, loose or even lost connections.

As a foreign rather than a domestic agency it is committed to an intelligence that is artistic rather than artificial. Artistic intelligence is looking for problems, not patterns. It is not interested in reoccurrences but deeply invested into recursive appearances: the paradox of a presence in absence and vice versa: absence in presence. By focusing on what is there without being recognized, what is seen without being visible, it mobilizes a self that does not learn from what is identified as usual but puts the ordinary to a test.

It is the foreign agency which allows to distinguish a temporary residency from regular employment or other forms of placement that are supposed to provide solutions or optimize processes according to established workflows and distributions of responsibility and ownership. As a laboratory where the setup is constantly changed with each temporary resident, a residency enables experiments based on the opportunity to 'call into question all that exists'.[7]

3

Artistic intelligence gives the researcher an assignment. The task is to intervene as a foreign agency into a local context and to transform the apparatus of research by challenging the predominant mode of knowledge production. Such a transformation means to question the current divisions of labour. On the most general level, it refers to the separation of manual from intellectual labour, productive from unproductive work, to knowledge based on reproducible and irreproducible data. This assignment is a call to leave the comfort zone, to break down the disciplinary silos and to radically re-imagine the all too familiar relationships between art and science, or art and technology.

The more an increasingly immaterial production is characterized by cognitive and affective forms of labour, the less distinct or transparent its inherited divisions become. Hybrid divisions replace the dichotomies of an industrial production that is based on the binaries of the either advanced or primitive character of a work. Genuinely composite forms of dividing tasks according to varying skills, expertise, ambition, and experience run across the former demarcation lines within production and operate transversally within established hierarchies of organization.

These divisions are constantly mirrored and carried forward in artistic production, although in distorted perceptions. It starts with the most obvious separations between applied and fine art, performative and visual art, and proceeds to more complex ones: divisions between text and image, fiction and documentary, craft and concept that are rooted in the compartmentalization of form and content, theory and practice.

Long before the advent of the post-industrial society, modernism and, in particular, contemporary art has anticipated hybrid relations of production that run across former divisions of labour, by criticizing, over-affirming, ironizing, or undoing them. It has become manifest in tendencies, movements, and schools such as Bauhaus, Brecht's epic theatre, pop art, but also conceptual art or relational aesthetics as well as a series of turns into various different directions, such as the pictorial turn, the performative turn, the documentary turn, and, most recently, the ontological or material turn.

Yet, even despite their intentions and explicit rhetoric, on a macro level these movements ultimately fail to address the most fundamental division between producer and consumer of art. As mirror images of each other, the hybrid perspectives of both consumerism and the creative industries become increasingly interchangeable. However, the fact that now everyone can act as if they are an artist does only further conceal the question of ownership of the means of artistic production. As Louis Althusser suggested, the challenge would be to reveal 'not the relations between the painter and his work, but the relations between a work and its painter'.[8]

On the micro-epistemological level of artistic research residencies there is not only a possibility but an urgency to reframe the question of ownership and to turn it upside down, precisely in the way Althusser suggests. Rather than conceiving it as a property relation, rather than understanding it as a relation between the artist and 'his' or 'her' work, rather than renewing the spiritual bond between authenticity and authorship, the actual challenge is to make visible in the artistic research process the invisible relations of knowledge production. This means to revaluate the abstract relations between a research and its practice, between new knowledge and its residence, or in the words of Althusser: a work and its artist.

4

As a preliminary conclusion, the potential of artistic research residencies could be revaluated according to three main aspects:

First, it introduces a notion of collaboration in a strange sense of the word: working together with a foreign agency. It is a collaboration that is not underpinned by sharing a common agenda. On the contrary, it encourages a mode of working that allows all involved parties to pursue their interests and ideas without first having to establish a general consensus or to synchronize according to the current divisions of labour. Rather than reproducing them, the ignorant view from outside onto the micro-economy of knowledge production in a local environment may work as a technique that discovers and explores the shortcuts, circumventions, and lines of flight as a way out of the ordinary divisions of labour. Such an understanding of collaboration is relevant to artist residencies in a generic sense, as well as to residencies that are embedded in specific contexts of knowledge production.

Secondly, artistic research residencies allow for the production of new forms of continuity. They attempt to connect the fragmented, temporary, transient, elusive, interfering, or resistant elements of knowledge in a non-linear process that creates a singular form of consistency at the intersection of research and residency. Rather than eliminating, discarding, or synchronizing them, the continuity of both research and residency consists of incompatibilities, heterogeneities, and discontinuities that run on trajectories that are 'distinct and incommensurable, yet complimentary'.[9] They have to be revaluated and recovered as the raw material of artistic curiosity, as unused resources or otherwise neglected capacities that can gain relevance in a new or innovative way.

On that basis it is possible to make a third claim. With the help of the concept of opacity, as it has been developed by Édouard Glissant,[10] it is possible to link the collaborative character of the residency with the non-linear continuity of artistic research. Opacity is the basic right of the creative or innovative process. It means to accept, rather than reject what cannot be understood. It acknowledges everyone and everything that is there, without constantly having to re-legitimate its presence. It embraces any possible and actual entanglement, but without limiting the possibility to question it all.

It is the residue that remains in residence, for ultimately the outcome in its entirety cannot be transferred, measured, or exchanged in an entirely reasonable fashion. Traces that link past and possible future research through inexplicable objects and unfinished lines of thought produce a more or less translucent layer of *not* knowing that it is saturated with uncertainty, contingency, ambiguity, openness, and surprise. Underneath this opaque surface, a reverse engineering of the apparatus of knowledge production can effectively take place.

Notes

1 Walter Benjamin, 'The Author as Producer', in *Selected Writings: 1927-1934 Part 2*, ed. Michael W. Jennings, Howard Eiland, and Gary Smith (Cambridge: Belknap Press of Harvard University Press, 2004), pp. 768-82, p. 774.

2 'Ek-stitutions exist: their main purpose is to come into being. They exist outside the institutional framework, and instead of infinite progress, they are based on a certain temporality.' Florian Schneider, '(Extended) Footnotes on Education,' *e-flux Journal* 14 (March 2010).

3 Platform 12 press release, 'Platform 12: Dialog between Research, Art and Business: Akademie Schloss Solitude and Wimmelforschung Robert Bosch GmbH', www.akademie-solitude.de/production/_files/file/admin/PM_Platform12_eng.pdf.

4 Larry J. Leifer and Martin Steinert, 'Dancing with Ambiguity: Causality Behavior, Design Thinking, and Triple-Loop-Learning', in *Management of the Fuzzy Front End of Innovation*, ed. Oliver Gassmann and Fiona Schweitzer, pp. 141-58 (Cham: Springer International Publishing, 2014).

5 Platform 12 press release.

6 Benjamin 2004, p. 770.

7 Ibid., p. 779.

8 Louis Althusser, *'Lenin and Philosophy' and Other Essays*, ed. Frederic Jameson, trans. Ben Brewster (London: New Left Books, 1971), p. 231.

9 Gilles Deleuze, *Cinema 2: The Time-Image*, trans. Hugh Tomlinson and Robert Galeta (London: The Athlone Press, 1989), p. 278.

10 Édouard Glissant and Betsy Wing, *Poetics of Relation* (Ann Arbor: University of Michigan Press, 1997), p. 189.

Antropofuga

Helmut Batista

> Schools that position themselves as privileged or exclusive sites of 'knowledge production' only reaffirm existing social inequalities and hierarchies.
> Paulo Freire

Long before we found a terminology for what we now call an art residency, artists and creators took part in immersive cultural experiences in different contexts. The Villa Medici is more than 400 years old and is probably the oldest art residency on the globe. When Da Vinci created his beautiful machines in some French castle, by invitation, he was probably in an art residency, as artists are today. He was earning his living and building up his CV.

Art residencies have not really changed from their core premise, which is to produce a 'different' time for production, materially or immaterially. Nevertheless, they have adapted to the ever-changing art context that reformulates itself according to so many different variables—economic, social, political, and so on. The spectrum of how contemporary residencies are conceptualized and run is immense, and some have become extremely 'elitist', while others seem to act more as occupational therapy programmes. This makes the endeavour of writing about residencies extremely difficult, if not impossible, as the existing models out there are just too diverse to be placed under the same terminology. Residencies have been growing in diversity much more than any other activity in the art world, in part due to cheap airlines and housing options, like Airbnb. Very few give you money. Many have become money-making services, enticing artists by making them think it will add to their CV. Some are used by galleries or biennials to save on costs, as transport and border control have made everything so much more expensive and time-consuming.

It is therefore important to understand from what context we speak about residencies, so that we do not dissect residency programmes into different administrational projects or understand them as a by-product of given specific economic and political conditions. As a counter point to Paulo Freire's above statement I would suggest: residency programmes, although they position themselves as privileged or exclusive and specific sites of 'knowledge production' should have as an underlying premise the desire to balance social inequalities and hierarchies.

Residencies as Educational Programmes

Julio Cortázar, in his brief text *Geografías*, has an interesting reconfiguration of the concept of Antropofagia: Antropofuga. Antropofagia has been widely explored and discussed and has its root in Brazilian modernism (Oswald de Andrade). Antropofuga (fuga = escaping), or escaping the Antropos (the human) is, in the context of this discussion, a very interesting concept. What kind of escape does a residency provide? And who is escaping from where or what? We escape because we need a change from the circumstances or the place that we are in. The reasons for this desire can be political, economic, social or any other issue. Often, we escape without knowing what we are looking for or even where we are going. It is a question of one's condition and development. For some it is a question of privilege; for others, it is a pure survival instinct.

From my understanding, there are two different ways of running residencies. One is born out of specifically local, and mostly individual, necessities. This is the case for Capacete, the place that I am writing from. It is also the case for other similar South-American programmes. The second version is that of an exchange programme built according to pre-established art politics and practices. Such programmes can be private or government-run. They vary according the organization's aims.

Rio de Janeiro, where I am based, is a city of 10 million people, of which only 40 per cent receive a sufficient education (according to European standards). The remaining 60 per cent of the population lives in squatted territories–the Brazilian shantytowns or *favelas*–and have no access to art education or even to art institutions. (As an aside, Brazilian art institutions are basically bankrupt, as a consequence of Brazil's neo-liberal American-style agenda. A residency programme does not make any sense under such circumstances. It is therefore no surprise that art residencies are more common in developed countries. Therefore, creating such a programme here in Rio confronts one to very different questions and problems.)

On a global perspective, it is not surprising that in recent years many residency programmes are considered or self-labelled as educational programmes. Many of them are indeed financed by governmental departments that view them as post-educational platforms. Lately, we have seen the rise of educational programmes all around the world that stand apart because they are not attached to any specific diploma, meaning you can define them as residencies, which are more open institutional structures by nature. Examples include: The School of Missing Studies, The School of Unlearning, The Night School, The School of Improper Education, The School of Everything, The School of School, The School of Death, The School of Redistribution, The School of Nature and Principle, The School of Narrative Dance and Other Surprising Things, The School of Improper Education, and so on.

The healthy rise in so many different programmes seems to show that a conventional art education, originated from the beaux-arts system, is no longer enough, and finds itself in a crisis. This is where such hybrid programmes come into play. Some more well-known examples include the Whitney programme in New York, Maumaus in Lisbon, De Appel in Amsterdam, SOMA in Mexico, PEI in Barcelona, and recently also the DAI in the Netherlands, among other short one- to two-year-long programmes. Since 2010, Capacete is also running something that remains deliberately undefined, and lingers in between a classical residency and an educational programme.

What unites these kinds of schools and residency programmes is that they deal with time in a very different way from other art world activities. Common grounds for some of these projects include the idea of listening, sharing as a form of construction, the organization of places for communal gatherings, and a non-hierarchical structure. Time is of the essence for this to happen in a very different way from what the neoliberal world is imposing on all productive systems.

Capacete gathers people as it gathers thought and time. It is by connecting people, by connecting thought through time, that it constructs its educational platform. It cannot be defined as a purely educational programme, and it also cannot define itself as a classical residency programme. It is somewhere in between or it is nowhere. Its undefined situation also reflects the difficult financial conditions one faces in developing countries such as Brazil.

The way Capacete runs its programme is very close to anthropology. Anthropology is a discipline that focuses on the study of human beings, in their ways of being, their interactions with one another and the world. It is a discipline that tries to keep everything in focus, and is therefore to some extent beautifully unfocused in its theories and obviously also in its approaches. Anthropological approaches are about listening, doubting, observing. Its methods are open-ended. In other words, time is the most valuable tool an anthropologist can have. In this sense, Capacete's programme can be described as an undefined experimental programme rather than an educational one, which would infer a specific pedagogical frame.

We believe that art is a tool for knowledge. It teaches us something in a specific way. Just showing up to an exhibition or a museum is educational in itself, beyond any explicitly pedagogical intentions, themes, or content.

That said, it is understood that an artistic practice is difficult to transmit. Art resists and its premise is to be against systematization. We are faced with an abundance of worn-out models from past eras, and the expectation and drive for profits, all of which are miles away from the practice of art itself.

Capacete: The Resident or the Residency, Who Is Hosting Whom?

As a residency or education programme it is important to understand and distinguish who we are hosting! We tend to throw all residencies into the same basket and then analyze what the programme has to offer. I believe the question has to be addressed differently: a programme should be designed to fit its residents, not the other way around. Capacete, in that sense, tries to adapt to its residents, rather than asking them to adapt to its programme. It is a platform for those professionals who have, somehow, still not found their voices in the art world or art market. Many of those professionals will end up leaving the arena of art production or research if life in that field becomes too difficult. Capacete is somehow designed for these professionals, giving them opportunities, while building other forms of knowledge production and sharing, and therefore expanding the possibilities of moving around in the field of art. We are talking here of professional people, mostly in their early (but often also late) thirties coming from different locations in the cultural arena.

Capacete provides intellectual and affective platforms based on potentially but not necessarily long-term collaborations. In its twenty years of existence, Capacete has been a hub for many of its ex-residents, providing them not just with a place to stay when they are in Brazil, but also assisting them in long-term projects, many of which would otherwise not be absorbed by the normal art market (galleries and institutions). These are often projects that simply take many years to realize. Capacete functions like a family for its multiple protagonists and works as a collective, without undermining individual voices. It collects voices and thoughts as if it were a family structure. Ex-residents can always come back (for free) if they feel like it, and if certain steps of their projects have not been fulfilled. Almost all seminars are done by ex-residents and ex-collaborators. This long-term investment and thinking are things you rarely find outside of a family structure. It is the opposite of the art market and the capitalistic modus operandi. As in family structures, we never know the limits of what can be offered and what can be asked for. It is this very undefined giving and taking that has an immense transformational power. We simply do not believe that you have to run to produce art. It is the function of a family to slow things down when real life is speeding you up.

The Open Call for the One-year Programme in Athens during documenta XIV

In early March 2017, Capacete landed in Athens, forming an approximately nine-month residency called Capacete Athens. With the thought of adapting its long-term modus operandi from South America to Greece, this 'gathering' of ten Latin American and two Greek participants (artists, curators, dancer, philosophers, and performers) framed itself as an experiment and proposed a first semester of listening, being together, engaging with documenta XIV and the local communities without necessarily having a goal. Actually, there were no imperatives in our proposition. That is to say, we were changing and being changed by being, by contemplating, and letting things happen. This was a programme without a programme. Perhaps this is the common point of some of the ideas that embrace the non-productivist use of time—to concentrate on being-together, on giving phenomena a chance to happen without pressure or imperatives.

The Proposal

Two main questions triggered the challenge to move to Athens. What does it mean to displace an experimental, collective, learning and research-based initiative from one continent to another, and specifically from South America to Southern Europe? What motivates such a dislocation, and what does it implicate?

How does such an initiative engage with a new local context and take into account the complexity and heterogeneity of its communities, histories, and socio-cultural dynamics? If, to some extent, ancient Greece was and still is used as raw material for shaping the imagination of Western modernity, what can contemporary Greece offer in dismantling colonialism and neoliberal, speculative, financed capitalism?

For twenty years, Capacete has received practitioners who were active in different fields and came from all over the world to experience, exchange, research, love, produce, present, publish, and share. Capacete's approach to learning and research is a time-based, collective, discursive, performative, and experimental practice that needs time and close involvement in order to produce a less hierarchical and more decentralized exchange and production system.

Structure of the Programme

The programme unfolded in two chapters for its twelve participants, each related to separate moments and conceptual frames. The first four months were dedicated to actively listening and seeing, starting prior to the opening of documenta XIV in Athens and continuing through its 100 days of exhibition. The focus of this period was to approach the local context by meeting local agents, practitioners, and institutions; as well as to establish bearings in the city and develop an intense conversational mode to approach current socio-cultural and political dynamics in Greece, and in Athens specifically. This period was also dedicated to understanding the entanglement between Kassel and Athens within the framework of documenta XIV. In order to achieve this, we also travelled to Kassel, and collaborated with local partners in Athens.

The second chapter, lasting six months, was dedicated to (re-)action. It began at the conclusion of documenta XIV in Athens and continued until December of 2017. During this period, different professionals–among them regular Capacete interlocutors, as well as local practitioners and agents in the Athenian context–were invited to collaborate with the selected group of participants in open, public programmes. This series of programmes had a specific theme: embracing the fact that dislocation generates questions (such as those posed above) more so than tidy thematic frameworks do. Our predicament was a case study that needed to be experienced in order to arrive at conclusions. Our interest was in how to react to the questions provoked by our given situation.

It's no surprise that the Athens group ended up spending a good portion of their time in Athens trying to understand what the hidden clauses in that open call were. Asking ourselves: who was hosting whom, why and for whom we were talking, where 'the project' ended and our lives began. Were we part of documenta XIV or was documenta XIV a part of us? Were Greeks understanding us as being part of documenta XIV or were we trying to make them understand that we were something else, that we were trying to escape any form of 'belonging to'? And how can such a displacement take place in a context so strongly produced and determined by documenta XIV? Does it make sense for us to produce something while the local population is being bombarded by its excess of manifestations and exhibitions?

A Temporary Conclusion: Antropofuga as Question, Antropofuga in Question

If production and productivity are the main determining factors in the current artistic context, then how can a school become a place for reclaiming spaces of daydreaming and non-productivity? One could identify this as a form of escapism, a moment of silence or a pause. What we are trying to attain is a form of learning beyond the imposed politics of time and productivity. Though we talk about a prototype for a school, a residency, education, or pedagogy, we are confronted with a fundamental question: how do we deal with the very precious tool we have, which is time, and what do we do with it?

And of course, these were not the only questions that were brought up: we also bonded, loved and fought each other, danced... and even wrote a bit. A publication was born out of this experience, which compiles some of the texts that resulted from the nine months we spent in Athens. Rather than a faithful (re)action to our experience, it is a chorale; a fragmented approach to the complexities and tensions in which we found ourselves immersed; an impossible cocktail of fun, family structure, confusion, unknown languages and micro-political challenges; a condition of being with and feeding from one other and from the multiple 'others' we encountered through seeing, listening, caring, offering, and thus living; a doing nothing, but doing a lot. Time and undefinition in its purest form.

Literature

— Cortázar, Julio. Historias de cronopios y de famas. Buenos Aires: Monotauro, 1962.
— Freire, Paulo. Pedagogy of Freedom: Ethics, Democracy, and Civic Courage. Lanham: Rowman and Littlefield, 1998.

Grounding Artistic Development

Maria Hirvi-Ijäs &
Irmeli Kokko

The common goal for most forms of artist residencies is to support and facilitate artistic development. This goal is also essential in EU cultural policy programmes such as in the *Policy Handbook on Artists' Residencies, 2011-2014.* Artists residencies are described there as a resource for professional development and as an investment in creativity. Residencies are thought to offer artists opportunities to develop ideas and connections, to get professional feedback, and to network. At the same time, they offer facilities for learning new skills and techniques. Additionally, residencies are expected to increase cultural awareness and competencies and to support organizational skills as well as personal development.

On Artistic Development

Artistic development often seems to be a self-evident abstraction that does not have much meaning as such and it is not clear either why residencies in particular would be suitable environments for it. In *Residencies as Learning Environments* (2015) Angela Serino justly poses the question:

> ... even the seemingly unproductive ones (like cooking a meal or exercising together) as an occasion to produce and put in circulation a specific knowledge that can eventually but not necessarily lead to a new work ... we would like to propose the idea of residencies as learning environments, and the residence period as a catalyst for processes of collective and personal (self-)development. By proposing such hypotheses, we ask: In which sense do residencies produce knowledge? If residencies really are learning environments, who learns from whom? What and how do we learn? Resident artists? Or are there also other figures or protagonists involved in such a process? (Serino 2015, p. 9)

How can artistic development then be understood and discussed? The qualities and characteristics of artistic development are not easily pinned down. It must be understood as a cultural and historical projection, which at the same time is entangled with the slippery concept of creativity and its potentially innovative functions. Still, it is essential to our idea of artistic practice, and greatly expected in the processes of cultural production. The evolvements of art have been documented and interpreted by art historians through analyses of works of art and their contexts, but the core of the process, the artistic development itself, often eludes these investigations.

In the research *Learning in Visual Art Practice* by the Swedish scholar Ann-Mari Edström has studied artistic development and learning processes in visual arts in three art academies in Sweden. This rare empirical study is based on repeated interviews among Swedish art students during the period 2001–2007. The central conclusion was that the most significant experience of learning happened in dialogic studio conversations. Furthermore, it became clear that the relation between artistic development and self-direction was essential. Self-direction requires self-defined goals and modes of realizations in an individually defined pace.

> The individual cases of studying that form the basis for the investigation represent a particularly autonomous and self-directing kind of studying ... which are largely qualities that characterize higher education in visual art practice in general. The focus of the study is on two aspects of dimensions of the development of the studies in visual art: the students' relations to their artwork, and to the use of studio conversations (Edström 2008).

In the study, artistic development was understood and defined as changes in the relation between the artist and the artistic work. The change is experienced at three levels of specific skills and competencies that ought to be gained in artist education for a possible artistic development. Edström uses the concept of 'resting assured', which is a question of confidence and trust. Only when this trust is achieved, it is possible to continue developing the artistic practice.

The first level identified by Edström is the relation with the closest sphere, oneself and the artwork: resting assured in the intimate. This means that there must be a trust in the artist's own creative ability and his or her own artistic expression. The second aspect is the relation to reality: resting assured in the uncertain. This means that the artist must be able to let go, and explore the unknown, no matter what. The third aspect is the relation to one's creative act: resting assured in the work process. This includes trusting one's own methods and proceedings in the different moments and elements of the artistic work.

To gain competencies and capabilities requires a personal state of trust in one' own ability and one's own work. Only then can it proceed, develop qualitatively, and become a professional practice. Pascal Gielen describes the same kind of procedure as building a bottom, a foundation, in an otherwise bottomless situation (Gielen 2015). This constant building process seems fundamental for continuous artistic development.

Residencies as Learning Environments

Edström's study was done in the Fine Art education context but there are significant similarities in Scandinavia between the situation of how artists live and work in the residencies and how students are thought to learn in art academies. Both in the residency context and in the Fine Arts education context visual artworks are understood as originally created by the practitioners. Creating something yourself is at the heart of understanding the visual artist's creative process. Like art schools, residencies aim at providing circumstances for this creation which is thought to be unique. Both in the Fine Arts educational practice and in visual art residencies the studio and what happens there forms the core.

Looking at artistic development through the format and function of artists residencies is one way to give the development a specific context. Residencies have become a significant part of the ecosystem of the visual arts and function as nodes in relation to different segments of different artworlds, cultures and markets. Within these art systems practicing professional artists face many collisions between the need for continuing artistic development and other cultural, economic, and societal expectations. The different kind of markets–be they commercial or non-commercial–ask for constant and instant production and seldom take the slower processes of development into consideration.

For this article we decided to conduct a micro-study on artistic development in residencies for visual artists. We interviewed artists at different stages in their careers and focused on how residency practices and experiences changed their own view on their art and on themselves as artists. The interviews were made 6–24 months after the residency, which had lasted 3–12 months.

As a theoretical background reference, we used the conclusions of Ann-Mari Edström's qualitative research. The idea was to bring tools from empirical and qualitative research to the discussion on artistic development in residencies.

Learning by Will and Necessity

> When I travel, I make the material I'm working with fit better in the conversation abroad, whereas in my home environment I am an outsider, as my practice is so different from the norm of practices at home, and the conversation really is not where I'm at; if there's a conversation it's more about whether your work sells or not. (Interviewee quote)

Artists residencies have potential as extended studies and learning environments and so they actually are. In addition, a growing number of residency programmes aim to function as a pro-longed transition from student to professional and focus on post-academic learning.

There are several common aspects between residencies and art academies. Historically, they share the same influences from the academy traditions in Florence and Paris (among others J-B Joly), the self-directed experimental art schools of the twentieth century such as Bauhaus, Black Mountain College or the IHEA, established by Pontus Hultén in Paris in the seventies. Self-directed modes of knowledge exchange are also a part of the activism and artistic development of the artists of today, as Helmut Batista describes in his article in this book. Informal gatherings and peer-to-peer meetings with other artists are essential to the self-assessment of one's work, also after graduating from formal academic training. Meeting with other professionals is part of a sustainable professional practice, of an ideal artist-biotope (Gielen 2014).

But unlike in art schools, residencies often take place abroad, in specific localities, with a simultaneous presence of other artists of various ages, career phases, and cultural backgrounds. When the residency takes place quite soon after graduation, the stay can be eye-opening and produce a shift in the artistic development. The fellow artists, the staff of the organization, and the local art scene form the site where the artist works during residency. The stories we heard show signs of vulnerability, both as an individual and as a practicing artist. The length of the time spent in the residency combined with a confrontation with difference, both in language, spoken discourse, and living environment, makes a wide variation of change possible.

> There were many artists in the group who had a long career behind them. It was great to see their enthusiasm. And it was wonderful that I could be in their company as an equal professional artist. The opportunity to work alongside artists of different disciplines and of different ages was very inspiring. (Interviewee quote)

Unlike at the art school, the heterogeneity of the artists group in terms of age, career phase and cultural background makes it possible to work and share knowledge without the sense of competitiveness that can easily beset students who all enter the professional life at the same time. Based on the interviews it is clear that dialogue and communication, without the element of competition, are foundational tools for artistic development.

One aspect that stood out in the material was the difference between coming to a residency with a clear working plan and a situation where the working process was open for new knowledge and development. Here the 'resting assured' in one's working process is put on test in combination with the resting assured in the uncertainty. Entering a residency without a clear idea of what one wants to reflect on or proceed with requires more confidence and trust in one's ability to develop artistic processes.

Another aspect concerns the fact that artists come from diverse and sometimes less privileged backgrounds. Then the importance of the residencies as gateways to learning is increasingly relevant. Possibilities for development, learning, and change may occur by being given access to information through libraries and other research sources, the availability of which cannot always be taken for granted. Depending on the outset, personal history, and socio-economic situation, residencies can provide access to knowledge and information, which will certainly have an effect on the artistic processes.

'By Invitation Only'–Privileged Laboratories?

Artist residencies are part of larger art ecosystems and are certainly not free from the hierarchies that characterize art markets in general. This can turn a residency into a process of navigating the power structures and the competitive nature of the professional setting. An artistic reputation also relates to stays in certain residencies and the residency network thus becomes one area where one take measures of an artists' status within the professional structures.

Residencies sometimes function as exclusive and differentiating mechanisms, which also can have negative effects on the artistic development. The interviews show that depending on the individual artists' situation, the experience of competitiveness can vary quite a lot. One part of the feeling of resting assured with the intimate, knowing oneself as an artist, is to know what kind of career to aim for and what efforts to make in the pragmatics of the artworld.

Residencies based on invitations work with curatorial tools in various ways. There may be implicit or explicit aims to promote certain directions of artistic development or to promote experiments by combining different art forms or modes of working.

Curatorial programming creates a substantial frame for a meaningful residency period. The first step in the curatorial process is the selection of residents. The group of peers, who share the time together, is an essential element of the artist residency, also in the long term. Afterwards, the experience of being able to contact peers in different parts of the world forms the foundation for working as an artist in the global-local context. During the residency, the group of peers is also the most important element in knowledge sharing and in discussions. An open call can, on the other hand, function as a sign of hospitality, giving everybody a chance to gain access to a certain environment to work in.

The conventions of selecting artists through open calls–short-listing, jurying, final selection–are challenged by digital developments. Artists are today actively shaping their own global communities and project networks via internet. This set-up can provide opportunities for new strategies: in her article in this book Donna Lynas describes how the changes in curatorial process of Wysing Arts Centre by including artists in the planning of the programme also changed the organization to adapt more dialogical practices. Self-direction, which is essential for artistic development, can have a positive impact already during the planning process of the residency.

There are certainly both pros and cons concerning the differences between open call systems and selection procedures based on invitations. A successful residency calls for strong, thorough, and at the same time flexible structures. This in turn requires structures for funding, secure processes, and quality assessments. It also requires long-term goals, expertise, and commitments from the organizers involved as well as from the artists-in-residence.

The resources and degree of support to artists at site are important, but at the same time it is a question of balancing the aims of the programme and the degree of collaboration and reciprocity.

International Networks and a Globalized Reality

The networking aspect is clearly relevant for artistic development but, again, depends on the situation. The residency organization and its role within the local art scenes is relevant wherever the residency is situated. In the best scenario the visiting artists have, through their presence and work processes, a great impact on the local art scene and can then function as a sphere of resonance for the local artists.

Networking is a complex notion with its political, cultural, and social dimensions. It should be understood not only as a network of connections between art professionals but also as an open point of connections between different regimes (Latour, Gielen, Van Maanen). It is a helpful tool for describing residencies as learning environments that differ from present-day educational institutions. Here the term is used to refer to both a process of making connections, and to being a point of connections in the context of residencies–between artists and art actors during and after the residency. On the other hand, reflected in the interviews of artists' experiences, the artists are not only in their own studios but also in a situation where connections can be hybrid. Not only the art institutions but also other regimes such as economical and educational knowledge systems are part of the temporary home situation in artist residencies. This is how the educational situation, compared to the time and space of art studies in universities, differs from artist residencies. When travelling to a residency the artist leaves not only her/his familiar and intimate relations behind but also the person and the artist as he/she is identified normally. Being together with other artists coming from different cultures and backgrounds forms the possibility for the new intimate in a temporary community. The artist can have a fresh start for 'living' and working. Professional curiosity and appreciation of other peers in the residency who don't have any idea of each other's position in their local artworlds is often a liberating experience, as was clear from the interviews.

Exposure, confrontations, and public appearances within the structure of a residency can function as an artistic tool for experimentation. By being in a different setting, the work is contextualized differently and can therefore be presented differently. This gives a new perspective of one's own work and on the methods of working. In one interview it became clear that the whole attitude towards and the understanding of the work mode changed during a longer stay in a respectable and well-resourced residency.

> The idea for my video work *Man in Blue Shirt* was fairly ready before taking off to my first residency. But the biggest significance of the Bristol residency came afterwards. It opened so many new thoughts and new perspectives for my work. During the last four years, when I've been in four residencies and lived abroad three years, my whole notion of art and making art has changed. My works before that were very inward-looking, but observing mainly my personal world started to change into observing life around me. The personal is still with me, but not as concretely as a subject matter. There's so much more interesting in the world than my inner world (Karjalainen 2010).

The key-experience, particularly of the first residency after graduation, is the experienced change not only in relation to one's own art but also to one's identity and in the relation between the self and the world. Residencies could be called hybrid networks of learning. A change in self-confidence and trust in one's own skills showed through a growing tolerance for critique in discussions. Or in new situations, such as negotiations with visiting gallerists when selecting artworks for a future show.

On the Doorstep to the Unknown

One main concept cherished in the residency discourse and in the interview material is 'open-endedness'. This carries several meanings, including no expectations of any results whatsoever. This means that artists needs to free themselves of the expectations implicit in the artistic work and the professional field, as part of the artistic development. To be able to handle this open-endedness means to see it as a reward in itself. This harks back to the foundational 'resting assured' in the uncertain as a professional capacity.

Open-endedness also refers to the relation of the artist to their own work. Organizers have witnessed how even the most experienced and established artists can find new relationships to their working process because of the open-ended mood in a residency. One artist talked about the process of 'stewing', of having the time to let whatever happens happen. Time is then not only seen as a support to the work process, but is appreciated as a significant ingredient of the artistic development.

Recognizing the differences and considering development in relation to production, it is possible to see residencies representing different value regimes (Gielen 2015). This means that they are valued and interpreted differently according to their aim. A product-oriented activity is performative, ready to show and trade. Development in turn is reflexive and investigative, delivering something else than exchangeable products. Both need time, but of a different kind, for different reasons and with different results.

This shifting between modes of processes leads to constant navigations and negotiations about time, for the professional artist. To build a foundation and to find confidence, over and over again, demands time. Artist residencies are seen as functioning as retreats here, as gaps in and of time. This make them sites of not only mobilized geopolitics, but also of what Sarah Sharma has named chronopolitics, the politics of time (Sharma 2017).

The concept and quality of time is obviously very central to the understanding of residencies. Time is seen as being without quality, a kind of post-time, with an exceptional duration (Ptak 2011). Time spent in residency is seen as a gap in regular life, a gap in regular time.

Time in artistic development seems to be related to not knowing what effects and affects experiences and non-experiences have. It is also a question of accepting this situation of not knowing and almost to seek it. This 'not knowing' what one chooses to do or not to do might turn into knowledge much later, even years after the residency stay. This awareness of time as an artistic ingredient very much clashes with the current cultural understanding of manageable time and controlled temporalities. Sharma's notion of chronopolitics identifies time as a structuring relation of power, in which the artistic insistence on time gaps could be developed into a mode of cultural resistance.

Transcultural Exchange–Intercultural Existence

On an individual level the process of cultural globalization has meant to become aware of differences between identities and of new forms of encounters in the dimensions of the local and the global.

Current residencies form a diverse international institutionalized web, in which artists from different cultures and countries travel from one place to another. Artists work and live various periods in international artists' communities, in new landscapes, other places and social settings, in other cultures and art worlds. Both human, urban, and natural environments; political situations, climates, landscapes, sounds, air, temperatures, animals and species of the particular residencies are part of the learning environment (Kokko 2008).

In a wider perspective, the artist residencies have a far-reaching potential in functioning as platforms for a locality and globality turning into glocality. A face-to-face interaction on site gives the cultural encounter a deeper dimension. This dimension has both practical and intrinsic effects on artistic development and on identity. It is also a clear channel for change in a wider perspective, in one's way of appreciating contemporary reality.

> During my first residency, which was in Mexico, I came to know a very interesting artists' group who had their own art gallery. Tourist industry of–in Mexico was similar to that in Kenya. Artists in Mexico fuelled their own art-scene; they built a collection, I realized that they could even, if working together, build a museum. Competition is hard in Kenya where I come from, and the history of thinking *I need help I cannot do it myself*–the idea that the black man is unable, comes from our grandfathers. It's very difficult to think *I'm black, I can, I'm able.* Mexico was a great example to me that you have to build your own art system. I saw that it's possible. (Interviewee quote)

Seeing something else, somewhere else, has been one of the basic learning experiences of artists' travels throughout the ages. Globalization takes different shapes in different locations and shows different amounts of transcultural exchange. With its activities the network of artist residencies is taking part in the practices of geo-culture, geo-politics and geo-economics. The artistic development can become political as such, or function as a tool for cultural negotiations.

Questions of time, money, cultural diversity and cultural rights are part of artists' reality and are foundational for artistic development. The network of artist residencies builds an intercultural existence in different degrees of institutionalized forms. Locations where political, economic, and social structures are taken for granted are paralleled, and can at best be combined, with less organized, more flexible, and less secure situations. The combined flexibility and transculturality seem to form a fruitful ground for artistic development.

The network of artist residencies functions also as an important communicative network with dissemination of information, knowledge, and discourses on contemporary art production and relevance. These channels of information are depending on your origin, contexts and artistic disposition, decisive for any kind of proceedings and development. Residencies have a significant role in developing platforms for transcultural learning.

Residencies in the Unknown

The idea of artistic development implies a need for change. Residencies are widely seen as having potential for qualitative alternative developments and artistic cultural diversification.

The role of artist residencies is significant for the development of individual artistic practices. A residency can provide an opportunity to discuss the artistic practices on a level that is not possible in less developed art scenes. For others, a residency can mean new settings that might not be as convenient as the personally developed private studio. This may lead to a different mode of working, networking, discussing, thinking, socializing, and exploring.

The empirical material used for this article, despite its modest size, gave a wide perspective on how residencies support artistic development. Summing up one can conclude that a successful residency cannot be guaranteed but development cannot be avoided. It is situation-specific and organization-specific. It also depends on the degree of experience and professionality of the artist, at least with regard to the navigation skills needed. The concept of 'resting assured' shows what is required. It is a question of confidence and trust. Only when this trust is realized, it is possible to continue developing the artistic practice.

Artist residencies seem to potentially be an alternative to the institutional and commercial structures of the art markets, mainly due to the fundamental ethics of open-ended time gaps and the implicit non-expectation. They are also potentially safe sites of non-regulated and free artistic development for anybody who needs it. Depending on the economic structures, residencies can also be seen forming another kind of art market in both a good and a bad sense.

Artist residencies, as facilitators of artistic development, may more and more become strategic fields of development in the arts and culture in general. As open and flexible structures, residencies may become a strong tool for (art) universities to link institutions of different regimes together. For instance, the Hub in London is a transdisciplinary research space within the Wellcome Collection where people from different backgrounds and with a wide range of expertise collaborate on projects exploring medicine, life, and art. The Wellcome Collection also provides interdisciplinary residencies for teams of scientists, visual artists, musicians, broadcasters, and clinicians to explore and shape perceptions and understanding of dementia. As a global research institute of health Wellcome Collection has also developed residency programmes in the context of medicine laboratories in Africa. One of the interviewees described this kind of residency experience as an 'extremely interesting and challenging project', where the position of artists-in-residence as outsiders enabled them to act as inventors of cultural communication tools between the researchers and local villagers. The artist also found this residency experience to be the way and the context she'd like to develop and practice in the future.

Residency programmes in a global perspective must be seen as self-directed learning environments for visual artists. The lack of qualitative research drives the national and international funding structures of the field of residencies towards demands for verifiable, often short-term outputs, along with the art market and the field of cultural services. Still, these communicative intersections between people, art, and culture may have a tremendous significance for artists in different career phases and thus for the development of contemporary art.

The main role of residencies in the long run seems to be that they form one answer to the growing importance of gaining time. Residencies are participating in the power structures of chronopolitics by insisting on using time as an ingredient and to let the gaps in time translate into art. However, residencies also act as learning environments for developing artistic practices outside of the studio-residency. This could be called an additional 'fourth level' of the three levels of artistic development identified by Ann-Mari Edström. The level of learning towards the world.

Literature

— Caro, Mario A. *Protocols of Engagement, Anticipating a Visit.* Unpublished talk, Res Artis Meeting, 18–20 June 2018.

— CCAUjazdowski Castle & AIR Laboratory, 2011. http://re-tooling-residencies.org/media/upload/img/ReToolingResidencies_INT.pdf.

— Edström, Ann-Mari. *Learning in Visual Art Practice.* Lund: University of Lund, 2008.

— Elfving, Taru. *Alternative Economies of Exchange.* Unpublished talk, Res Artis Meeting, 18–20 June 2018.

— Gielen, Pascal. 'Safeguarding Creativity: Institutional Insecurities of the Artistic Biotope in a Global Market Orientated Europe.' In *Handbook of Cultural Security*, edited by Yasushi Watanabe, pp. 398–417. Cheltenham Glos: Edward Elgar Publishing, 2018.

–. *The Murmuring of the Artistic Multitude: Global Art, Memory and Post-Fordism*, Amsterdam: Valiz, 2009.

— Hutchens, Jessyca. *A Gift of Time: The Residency as Retreat.* Unpublished talk, Symposium Saari Residency, 17 June 2018.

— Kokko, Irmeli. *Taiteilijaresidenssien rooli nykytaiteen tuotannossa.* Jyväskylä yliopisto: University of Jyväskylä, 2008. http://urn.fi/URN:NBN:fi:jyu-200807015572.

— Maanen, Hans van. 'From Theory to the Methodology of Singularity: Bruno Latour and Nathalie Heinich.' In *How to Study Artworlds: On the Societal Functioning of Aesthetic Values*, pp. 83–104. Amsterdam: Amsterdam University Press, 2009.

— Majava, Antti. *What is the Future of Art, Science and Technology Residency Programmes?* Panel discussion, Res Artis Meeting, 18–20 June 2018.

— *Mapping Residencies* no. 2, 2015. http://mappingresidencies.org/en/.

— Ptak, Anna, ed. *Re-tooling Residencies: A Closer Look at the Mobility of Art Professionals*, Report on Building a Strong Framework for Artists' Mobility: *Five Key Principles.* Working Group of EU Member States' Experts on Mobility Support Programmes, 2011. http://ec.europa.eu/assets/eac/culture/library/reports/artist-mobility-report_en.pdf.

— OMC Working Group on Artist' Residencies. *Policy Handbook on Artists' Residencies: European Agenda for Culture: Workplan for Culture 2011–2014.* S.l., 2014. http://ec.europa.eu/assets/eac/culture/policy/cultural-creative-industries/documents/artists-residencies_en.pdf.

— Sharma, Sarah. 'Speed Traps and the Temporal: Of Taxis, Truck Stops, and TaskRabbits.' In *The Sociology of Speed: Digital, Organizational, and Social Temporalities*, edited by Judy Wajcman and Nigel Dodd, pp. 131–51. Oxford: Oxford University Press, 2018. http://sarahsharma.com/wp-content/uploads/2018/01/Speed-traps-and-the-temporal_Sharma.pdf.

— Serino Angela. *Residences as Learning Environments*, [Milan:] FARE, 2015. www.farearte.org/wp-content/uploads/2016/01/International_Meeting_of_Residences_light.pdf.

Interviews

- Huuskonen, Juha Helsinki, August 2018
- Kyambi, Syowia, Helsinki, March 2018
- Laitinen, Tuomas A Helsinki, April 2018
- Linna, Meri, Helsinki, April 2018
- Olsson, Daniela, at Wellcome Collection in London, May 2017.
- Pääkkönen, Maria, Helsinki May 2018
- Pousette, Johan, Stockholm May 2018

Part 3

Institutional and Artistic Reflections

Residencies as Programmatic Spaces for Communality
An Interview with Nina Möntmann

Irmeli Kokko

Irmeli Kokko – You have a background as a curator at the Nordic Institute for Contemporary Art, NIFCA (1997-2007), in Suomenlinna, Helsinki from 2003-2006...

Nina Möntmann – At NIFCA we had a global residency programme, with a focus on residencies in the Nordic countries and a couple of collaborations with residencies all over the world, such as Khoj in Delhi or Arts Initiative Tokyo, where Nordic artists could go. There was also a geographic focus that changed every couple of years. When I was there it was the Baltics, before the UK.

Our offices were located on the island of Suomenlinna in Helsinki, where we always had four or five artists in residence at a time, which also offered an opportunity for long-term collaborations with artists on expansive projects, including them in organizing and participating in workshops, events, and so on. This residency model of sending Nordic artists around within the Nordic countries and globally, and in return inviting a few artists from other geographic regions to the Nordic countries was very much related to the politics of the Nordic Council of Ministers, the funders of NIFCA.

Many of the Nordic residencies are very family-friendly, supporting travel for partners and children and providing larger apartments equipped for families or handicapped artists and support single parents in finding childcare, which should be standard. Otherwise you not only exclude a lot of artists, but also suggest or support a special way of living and career building, willingly or not: the young, healthy, always flexible artist, independent of any personal commitments, which also matches a neoliberal concept of work and, of course, also caters to the demands of the art market. Those residencies, when they don't provide significant funding and support or a programme relevant for the artist's work and development, run the risk of becoming just another station in the self-managing and often precarious career of an artist. Likewise, for artists' collectives the conditions of residencies could be improved in many cases. And stipends need to be attached to residencies as a standard, which is, unfortunately, far from the real situation. Without a stipend, artists risk precarity, when leaving their routines, day jobs, and so on for a residency.

IK – The world has changed rapidly. Do you believe that artist residencies based on a travelling artist model will continue as a mainstream residency model?

NM – Some of the issues of the 'travelling artist model' as you call it are still valid, even if they may not appear as the most urgent ones today: many of the younger artists, after having left art school, are eager to get to know the art scenes in other places, have experiences and meet other artists, curators, and critics, see a lot of exhibitions, attend film festivals, and so on. For them it can be very productive to spend a few months in another place and experience art production in a different context far away from the context they are familiar with. Following the same model, for more established artists the needs and demands for a residency change and they might seek the best conditions to realize a bigger project, or to use a residency as a support for a specific research. For young curators a residency can offer the first opportunity to curate an institutional exhibition and to have access to a wider public.

To my mind there is a development that is going in a different direction. Although these more traditional residencies will continue, because they can provide the resources needed for artist-driven production and curatorial experimentation, there is a more programmatic model emerging, which uses the residency as a platform for collective research, debate, and action. Here the hosting institution serves as a tool and a catalyst for political demands formulated by cultural producers within a rising right-wing nationalist political climate. Scheduled by the hosting institution as well as by resident-driven programmes around topics such as climate change, sexism, fascism, and exclusion this can facilitate the breeding ground for creative resistance from and within the cultural field. Les Laboratoires d'Aubervilliers in Paris, for example, recently produced several closed events following that direction.

IK – If we look at the multiple organizations of contemporary artist residencies as institutions with their own (Western known) history, professional practices, mission, and values, the obvious difference with other art institutions is their relatively free status as public interests. Until now, residencies have managed to keep their fairly distant and self-determined role in the institutional art field and public sphere. How would you describe the present position of contemporary artist residencies in the ecosystem of art?

NM – I got the impression that on the one hand many institutions, also educational ones, are interested in offering residencies, in order to affiliate artists with their own practice and profile. In many cases the intention is to integrate them temporarily into their activities, such as a research platform or a large-scale project. On the other hand, these residencies often are underfunded and don't provide a lot of support to the artists, researchers, or curators. With many institutions suffering under tough economic conditions, residencies often are cut to a minimum, not necessarily in number, but in production budgets or fees.

But no residency programme is the same, there is no fixed protocol for how to structure and organize a residency and there are no generalized expectations for a specific outcome. As part of the artistic field, where institutions are more and more caught in the doom loop of obligatory managerialism, fundraising, reporting, and meeting the expectations of public and private funders, residencies can use exactly their undefined profile to provide an open space for untargeted thinking and experimentation.

Another claim for residencies can be that they can be a kind of sanctuary space for people who are expelled elsewhere: artists, curators, and writers from countries that don't support culture or even oppress or censor culture. Relating to the specific situation in the US, Laura Raicovich in a recent article took this idea even a step further and demanded of museums in countries rejecting refugees and asylum seekers, that they open their doors for those whose existence is criminalized by the state.[1] A future-oriented residency today has to go beyond the traditional parameters and use residencies to create a social space that counters authoritarian politics.

IK – What role and meaning can residencies have for art/artists today?

NM – Just like most curators are longing for more time for research, which only takes approximately 10 to 20 per cent of their time besides fundraising, management, and cultivating sponsors, many artists are caught up in a spiral of permanent productivity as requested within a neo-liberalized art system, and would wish for more time to just think and experiment. Stepping outside of the economy of recognition and leaving the routines for a residency in another place could provide this space for thinking. If this residency then works with a proper fee and production budget, it can avoid the risk of precarity, which I mentioned before.

Some residencies offer residency/summer school hybrids, for example the Nida Art Colony in Lithuania, which also foster collective experimentation and exchange. Experimental think tanks for temporary communities are a model that refers to seventies ideas of a residency retreat, which in those times often took place in nature. Adapted to the current situation of a changing world system and the question of how collectivity could be lived and defined in a way that matters, residencies can develop models of communality and provide temporary spaces to experiment with these ideas. As collective retreats they have the potential to reflect how people can organize as a collective to potentially transform an interest group into a collective production or political project. Today the aspect of going public is gaining great importance, of using residencies as temporary retreats to work under unregulated conditions and develop bold and risky ideas on how to creatively have an impact on societal developments.

IK – Can you elaborate a little on this collectivity? In what ways do you see collective production as potential for transformation?

NM – A major topic several disciplines are doing research on and are experimenting with at this moment is figuring out what forms of collectivity could matter or have an impact on future societal developments. Even with a left populism as defined by Chantal Mouffe and Ernesto Laclau, the model of commons or solidarity as a basic principle seems to be the central value of how to live together.

But living together doesn't seem to be sufficient at this crucial moment in history, when the world system of neoliberal finance capitalism is collapsing and the terms of another are still to be negotiated. As Immanuel Wallerstein has put it, a new world system will be installed by 2050, and we are facing violent times until then. The question is, how can we participate in these struggles in a non-violent way? How can it matter what we are doing as artists, curators, researchers, when it comes to negotiating a new world system not based on profitable economics and nationalisms, but on equality, well-being, and ethical relations within micro as well as macro systems?

Collective residencies and collective work in general can give us a frame not only to negotiate but also to practice more ethical models of relations: exchange instead of competition, solidarity and respect for others. This might sound a bit of a heavy load for an artist residency to deal with, but what I mean is more about building a consciousness and a practice of sharing as it can happen within a safe space and an open situation. So that when you make political claims you know what you are talking about.

IK – You have recently researched the current situation of small art institutions in the Nordic context. What are the key tendencies in the changing role and practices of small institutions? As many residencies fit into this category, do you see the current challenges and significance of residencies resonating with those of other small institutions?

NM – I see few corresponding tendencies in small-scale institutions and residency programmes. The proximity of small-scale and medium-sized institutions to their local audiences and places is an example, and the corresponding specificity of artistic and curatorial activities, which engage people to participate on a local level and learn from an international or global perspective. These perspectives are also crucial in residencies, when they gather artists, curators, and other cultural workers from various parts of the world, while supporting a local engagement. Small-scale institutions as well as some residencies encourage people to participate both as individuals and as part of a community.

In that sense, these institutions create an active public sphere. While large museums reach out to audiences, smaller galleries generate publics, constituencies or contact zones. Many residencies create these contact zones as the core of their activities.

These activities could benefit from public support that recognizes the civil qualities and benefits being produced. However, these institutions are increasingly struggling with insecure, short-term funding and unnecessary managerial effort. Instead, politicians and stakeholders should recognize and support small and medium-sized art institutions as resources for learning and the creation of civil society. In that sense, residencies, as part of the programme of a small-scale institution or as an individual institution, could also benefit from public recognition as platforms for participation in civil society, education, or the rights of women and migrants.

This interview took place via email between 2 October and 18 October 2018.

Note

1 Laura Raicovich, 'Why in the Age of Trump, I Believe the Art World Must Become a Sanctuary', Frieze.com, 14 March 2018, https://frieze.com/article/why-age-trump-i-believe-art-world-must-become-sanctuary.

Inspiration

Patricia Jozef

One day, a man goes to see his doctor: 'Doctor, I suffer from inspiration.' He tightens his diaphragm and draws air into his lungs.
The doctor looks worried. 'I'll have a look', he says. With a stethoscope he checks whether the breathing sounds are normal, reduced, or absent.
'An anomaly', the doctor concludes.
'As I suspected', says the man.
'You are not the only one. Around one third of my patients suffer from some stubborn or mild form of inspiration. They have too many good ideas but their hands are paralyzed. Rapid diagnosis and treatment of the underlying cause gives the best chance of avoiding further complications. Nothing has been lost.'
The doctor then examines the hands of the man. He touches his arm. 'But here you've got a strong gold vein, and I see that you have already tapped it several times.'
'Think, doc, and help me.'

After a silence, the doctor says: 'You might be carrying something with you, you might be carrying a weight on your shoulder. Do you sometimes smell an old man's breath or a specific perfume? Your teachers, where are they? Are they still sitting on your shoulder after so many years, looking at what you are doing, every letter, every word, every new idea that you put on paper hesitantly? Is there still a teacher whispering in your ear: "Can you explain to me what you mean by this?" Or does he stay silent, with a deep frown, in an S-shape, the S of skeptical? Do you still think your teacher is right? One morning you wake up and realize that your teacher was a person who works and earns a living, who sets his alarm clock and gets up grouchy in the morning.'
'Thank you, Doc, but I am there already. I did learn to live with that thought. Powerful, beautiful but frightening as well, perhaps even too huge to bear. I know that I'm free.'

The doctor nods thoughtfully. 'What does a normal day for you look like? For example: What have you done today?'
The man says he has frequently checked Facebook, and is well aware of what is going on in the world.

When asked if he has posted anything himself, he answers: 'A picture of the spelt bread that I baked this morning.'
'How many likes?', the doctor asks.
'230'
'Not bad.'
'I know. I try to keep my profile vibrant. Whenever I have something essential to post ...'
'Spelt is a bit passé', says the doctor. 'Try a paleo bread next time.'

They both shift into thinking.
'No walks', the doctor advises. 'Avoid the forest. It is the place of lavish good air and copious ideas. For you in no way a place to abide.'
'Are you crazy?', the man says. '1 + 1 = 2. The linear unit of the words. Like I would be someone to lose myself in a tree. That binary logic. One becomes two, two becomes four. I do not want to stick to that basic idea of classical thought. I prefer to go underground, for example in a cave where rats crawl over each other, crawling in all directions. A large rat cave as a complex of interconnected tunnels, cavities, and passageways. Rat caves are unsteady. They become larger when new residents come to dig new tunnels and close old ones. Any point can be connected to any other point. The principle of heterogeneity, doc.'
'Gilles Deleuze, isn't it?'
The man concedes.
'Isn't Deleuze also becoming passé?', says the doctor. 'Let it go.'

'Where were we?', the doctor picks up the conversation. 'All of old.'
'Yes, nothing else ever,' the man moans.
'Ever tried?', the doctor asks. 'Ever failed?'
In the silence that follows, the doctor reads the answer. 'No matter. Try again.'
'And fail again? I cannot do better, doc. Beckett rejected optimism, I can 't handle that.'

It seems that the doctor is now also being carried away by the thought of the hopeless misery, futility, and loneliness

of human existence.
But then the man's eyes light up when he says, 'Maybe I can become a second Roland Barthes.'
'Tell me more.'
'For his entire life Barthes prepared a novel that he would never write.'
'Do you collect your notes about that? This could be interesting.'
The man has to answer in the negative.

'What is your aspiration?', the doctor asks.
'I would like for a visible existence to be granted to that what the untrained seeing considers invisible.'
'The magical theory of seeing-in-practice.'
'I could also become a visual artist. I have always dreamt of creating images', says the man. 'In a large studio. With a wooden floor, a copper latch and a golden light. And an espresso machine.'

They let their thoughts go back and forth, the man and the doctor, about the benefits, about the immediacy of an image and, in contrast, the slowness of a text. About the writer and the limited range of a book written in his small language area and the international opportunities of the visual arts. About easy money that can be earned with a single painting.
They almost come to something, an upbeat thought, a plan and a possible breakthrough, a start for the day of tomorrow, a solution, an active package in which the surplus of inspiration could finally manifest itself in a sublime product, when the man says: 'What is the sense of all of this? What chances do I have left in these days when I am discriminated against as a privileged, heterosexual, middle-aged, white man?'

The man looks out the window at the quiet sky.
'Are you crying?', asks the doctor.
'No, I looked at the lines planes are drawing in the air and I was blinded by the bright light.'

He pays and leaves the room.

Inspiration.

The word carries all the romance daily practice lacks. As if it were a separate part of a human being, or a moment in time: a genius inspiration that must be released immediately and realized before it evaporates.

The muse as a source of inspiration.

The nine goddesses of art and science who are called upon to ask for inspiration, before embarking on a creative act. The muse of the hymn, the song and lyricism, of the flute, of the heroic epic, of philosophy and rhetoric, the muse of historiography, of the tragedy, of sacred songs, dance and lyrical poetry, of comedy, of astronomy.

They are called Erato, Euterpe, Kalliope, Thaleia or Urania and all of them mean something that enters the space of languorous dreams: sweet, the one who brings pleasure, soft-voiced, flourishing or heavenly. Dressed in long robes, concealing, but not too much. The eyes are raised to heaven or modestly lowered.

The muse is a woman. Sweet words whispering. A beautiful, inspiring woman, quiet and in the background, soft in nature. Her body is pillow-soft and smooth. She does not have a shrill voice and she does not fart.

So far for the romantic idea of inspiration. It is over-estimated. Having had that idea, the work has not yet been done.

What follows that small injection we could call inspiration, is the necessity of TIME and SPACE.

Time: the many hours that go into the creative process, the unspectacular hours of labour in a studio. These many, many hours, described by Hannah Arendt as: dilettant tinkering, grotesque overconfidence and ever returning doubt in the studio. Doing, working, trying, practicing, repeating, playing, failing and succeeding.

Space: the artist's studio as a violent and holy place. I am not aware of any other place where violence and quality are that close as in the space of the studio.

Violence: making 10 drawings, destroying 7 of them. Writing the first 60 pages of your novel, deleting 45 of them. Holy: I don't know any other place in the world where I can demolish so much without causing harm to someone.

Violence: I am failing, again and again, and I don't get it, whether it is a technical issue or an idea for which I do not find the right form. Holy: Do I know any other place where deficiency and ignorance can exist without being punished?

Violence: in front of me there is the empty sheet, this vast plain of possibilities without signposts where I get lost time after time. It's so lonely. Holy: is there any other space where I can invent rules at my own discretion, where I do not have to live up to expectations and where the undefined has so much authority?

One of the most beautiful words, in the context of creation, in Dutch is: 'eigenzinnig'. Literally translated 'own-sense'. It means: following something motivated by a vague sense of meaning. Or following something by a strong belief of sense. It is hard to find the right translation for 'eigenzinnig'. Both in Dutch and in English, most of the so-called synonyms are loaded with negative connotation: stubborn, obstinate, headstrong, but also bossy and even lunatic or moon-sick.

A moon-sick day in the studio, there are less poetic descriptions of a typical working day.

An *intelligent accident*, some call the work of Raoul De Keyser.

We never witnessed the real accidents, the terrible failure that preceded his most touching oeuvre. And I do not regret that. There is the intimate production time in the artist's studio, and there is the audience, which has no insight in this inappropriate and unprecedented studio-time.

Everything can be justified afterwards, when it has become radiant because of those many pairs of eyes that raised it to a higher level.

> Now banality shines.
> Confirming hum.
> Approving nod.
> Long live the audience. And: fuck the audience.

When I work, when I write, I want everyone out. Out of my mind, out of my thoughts. And if possible, I also want to forget myself: that unstable palisade of the judgmental, ashamed, or desiring self.

The judgment is an echo of a possible audience. Also fantasmatic. As well as one's own thoughts attributed to another. Anyway, the audience should be on time, preferably not too early.

Shame. Hell yes. Here and now. Shame is whispering humiliating words that only I can hear. But in the closed space of a studio, shame is not welcome.

Desire, that too. The worst of the three, because it has many graceful forms. An audience full of expectations is one thing... but dammit, that expectant, well-camouflaged father could be among them.

To conclude this plea for private studio working time, I would like to quote Coetzee. In his acceptance speech for the 2003 Nobel Prize in Literature, he recalls his parents, hoping to notice they are proud, after so many years of labour.

'For whom', he said, 'do we do things that lead to Nobel Prizes if not for our mothers. Mommy, mommy, I won a prize! That's wonderful, my dear. Now eat your carrots before they get cold.'

In the Margin of a Marginal Segment
An Interview with Jean-Baptiste Joly

Irmeli Kokko

Irmeli Kokko – Miwon Kwon suggested in her book *One Place after Another* (2002) that the role of residencies has been to provide 'landing places' for the new mobile creative class in the globalizing artworld. Can you go along with this interpretation about the ethos behind the emerging residencies of the nineties? To make spaces and routes for connections, new social formations in the new world situation?

Jean-Baptiste Joly – Seeing the role of residencies as providing 'landing places' for the new mobile creative class in the globalizing artworld? Yes, this is something I can totally agree with. This happens indeed worldwide at the moment, especially in South-East Asia and in the Pacific area. Almost every small town thinking about its future is opening an artist residency, understood as well as a tool for developing new creative economies and to prove that they belong to this new world. The end of the Cold War had (indeed) a real influence on the development of artists residencies. In Eastern Europe, many were created in empty buildings, in historical monuments used by the former socialist nomenklatura, or in former administrative buildings and schools, like for example in the Ujazdowski Castle in Warsaw.

For Akademie Schloss Solitude the fall of the Iron Curtain happened in the year when it was created. After November 1989 we immediately looked for contacts in the German Democratic Republic and invited artists from Eastern Europe, who could finally travel, to apply for the new fellowship programme at the Akademie. Somehow, this first social and political engagement became a strong part of our identity. We provided GDR-artists with travel fellowships in order to help them to discover Europe, offering them our contacts and addresses in London, Rome, Paris, or Dublin. We continued this travel fellowship programme in the nineties with artists from Ukraine, Lithuania, and Poland. After 1999 we initiated step by step a new kind of cooperation and exchange with NGOs in Warsaw, Budapest, Sofia, Belgrade, and Zagreb, trying to make this collaboration equal for both sides, not patronizing (from our side). On the one hand this Western-Eastern European dialogue was one of the priorities of the state of Baden-Württemberg, on the other I felt personally committed by the question of a possible European integration, seen from the perspective of the development of new artists networks. The reason why I felt so much involved in this matter–if I may be more personal–is that I, as a French baby-boomer, had the chance to be part of the new experience of French-German friendship of the sixties, as a student in secondary school and at university, as a teacher in France and in Germany, as director of a French Cultural institute in Germany. So I strongly felt my debt towards this and wanted to give something back to others in the new context of an open continent.

IK – How would you describe the role of residencies today, compared to the nineties? Is the basic model of residencies as it has been, still suitable?

JBJ – After the warm-up round you now come with very heavy stuff! 'Is the basic model or residencies as it has been still suitable?' Not so sure about this question because there is no real basic model if you compare current residency programmes with how it was at the very origin–should we go back to reasons why the Académie de France in Rome was created in 1666? Or to the different ways artists colonies of the nineteenth century influenced the invention of residencies all over the world? If we look at this from a more abstract perspective we could say that an artist residency is combining a person (the 'artist'), a space (the 'residency') and a defined segment of time (the 'sojourn').

The question is not easy to answer because these three variables have considerably changed over the last thirty years. Compared to the late eighties, the definition of the artist is a different one, it now includes activities that were not considered art in the past, or did not even exist; the clear distinction between artist and non-artist is somehow blurring. Also, the notion of space (the residency) is permanently questioned by virtual reality, so that we can be somewhere else without leaving home, diminishing the necessity of moving to a remote residency to experience otherness. Regarding the notion of time in the last decade I experienced its permanent acceleration with the fellows of Akademie Schloss Solitude. They often ask to split their residency in shorter segments, taking options about the future but making no decision, and having the permanent desire of being at different places at the same time. These fundamental changes in the daily life of a residency have to be taken into consideration. For this reason, in 2002 we opened a new section dedicated to the dialogue between art, science, and economy, in an area of activities where a start-up and an artist studio might be more or less the same, where artistic and scientific research might be close to each other, where activities can grow to a new business model or to an art project, where there is no difference anymore between working and hanging around. Three years ago, we opened a virtual academy, called 'Schlosspost', supporting with micro-fellowships web-residents we will never meet in the real world and hosting their projects and activities on this online platform. Compared to more traditional cultural institutions with a clear and limited definition such as museums (conserving and going public) or theatres (producing on stage and going public) artists residencies have a very favourable position because their task is rather vague: For this reason artists residencies, which are extremely flexible and versatile, are places that should be able to adapt to new artistic practices and new challenges and to rethink the relationship between the artist and the institution, i.e. between the artist and the society.

IK – Yes, my question covered only the very recent history of residencies. With the 'basic model' I meant the way residencies have been organized internationally since the eighties-nineties (or maybe from the seventies onwards?). And also their core mission, which is to provide time and space for artistic development, to test and to experiment. How could residencies support artistic work in the future in a sustainable way in an environment that is so governed by creative economy and growing art markets? Has the notion of time as a quality without expectations–with undefined results–become incompatible with the demands artists are facing?

JBJ – For sure one of the priorities for artists residencies is to maintain a space that allows 'a detour for nothing', as

French philosopher Fernand Deligny defined art and artistic practice in the fifties. At the moment, at least in Europe, I don't know any residency that would be so close to the art market that this would influence its way of working. By the way, only a very small percentage of the practice of visual artists is ending in an object that might have a value on the market. What I know from my experience in Solitude is a practice that is in itself an artistic intention, leaving behind the old-fashioned notion of 'a work of art'. As you know, the main incomes from the art market are generated by antique handicraft, ancient furniture, and painting. The most expensive artists on the art market are dead artists. And in the last small segment left for living artists the market is dominated by the 500 names mentioned in different magazines with long lists ranking names and prices. The majority of them is based in China, which represents already 37 per cent of the world art market today. In this context artists residencies are working in the margin of a marginal segment.

And even more important: your question implicitly reduces the artists hosted in a residency to visual artists! Too often artists residencies are identified with visual arts. But artists residencies don't only offer opportunities to visual artists. What about performing arts, literature, architecture, sound and music, and many other artistic disciplines? There is no other place where, artists can work with a collective, invent new practices, and experiment with new interdisciplinary practices without the immediate pressure of public success. Indeed, the current cultural production (performance, literature, music, cinema) is led by a logic that induces public success: the tyranny of the number of visitors. What I could imagine for the future would be the creation of a new kind of small artists residencies hosted by cultural institutions (theatre, opera, museum, Kunsthalle, publishers, and so on), hosting artists for a couple of months who could work and experiment freely, with a possible option for a production that could take place (but not necessarily) years later, without the dangerous temptation of an immediate return in terms of economy of media recognition.

You also mention in your question the creative industries. At the level of the European Union this dimension of culture is now recognized as a crucial dimension for getting public funding and it endangers the whole cultural production, not only the work of artists residencies. This means that the new understanding of culture expressed by the European Union is now including creative industries. Officially, the cultural budget has increased but on the other hand the funding dedicated to cultural projects closer to the classic artistic disciplines is decreasing. Through this decision and policy, culture as we understand it is becoming even more marginal. If an artist residency wants to have access to this new funding they have to follow the new rules and explain under which conditions the project they might apply for is including creative industries. A dangerous evolution, I would say, against which a few professionals protested but this was never a major topic for press and media.

IK – Yes, I agree with you that all art disciplines should be considered when discussing residencies. But because of the fact that most artists residencies in Europe are still for visual artists, the discussion of residencies tends to be focused in visual arts. And also a discussion from a European perspective only, which has no other logic than that two Europeans are now discussing it.

Would you regard residencies as testing and development grounds for cultural production? Or, depending on how you define 'culture', maybe no longer only for cultural production but also as societal testing grounds? Artists residencies can be used as an instrument for almost anything when starting new operational models in any field. What would be your next new start within the artists residencies in 2020s?

JBJ – As said before, artist residencies are flexible and versatile, and therefore they are also not normative. A residency can be almost anything, including the classical European way of thinking about it, with the classic artists studios, facilities implemented in a historical building, financed by public funding, as defined before 1989 with residencies such as Bethanien in Berlin or Tyrone Guthrie Centre at Annaghmakerrig in Ireland, or even Akademie Schloss Solitude. In the meantime, you find many other types, in

Europe or elsewhere, nomadic residencies through Cambodia, ephemeral ones for a couple of weeks around a specific topic, like for example an environmental project on the seaside in Taiwan, occupations of a former shop in a social housing building in Manilla, or even a single room in a private apartment. I really love this extreme diversity of the notion of hosting artists that can take any form of space under the most varied conditions. In the future, all these kinds of residencies will co-exist side by side, involving hospitals, universities, companies, some affirming the current state of the world, some being involved in a political or ecological or gender struggle. In the early seventies, the Belgian artist Marcel Broodthaers was using the metaphor of the winter garden to describe the role of a museum, considering that art is kept in a safe space like exotic plants in a winter garden, because this is not the right season to expose them to the outside world. In the same sense, pieces of art overwinter the bad season, waiting for the moment when art may again survive in a natural, open environment. When I see flourishing residencies and new initiatives growing everywhere, my idealism tells me that it now might be the time when, through the development of residencies, artists are everywhere, implementing art outside of the museum. Though one might have so many reasons of being pessimistic, this makes me rather optimistic.

This interview took place via email between 14 December 2017 and 18 January 2018.

Part 4

Art Ecosystems

Challenging the Sense of Time and Space

An Ethical Confrontation in Artist Residencies

Francisco Guevara

Time and space are sine qua non for artist residencies. Although residency models and their roles are numerous and diverse, especially considering their different contexts and missions, anyone around the world who engages with residencies is confronted by the question of time and space. From the perspective of residency owners and managers, and in a practical sense, in terms of resources, the questions of place and duration are always primary considerations. Also, in the process of selecting a location and developing an artistic intention, artists will decide based on the variables of space and length of time. Even when we approach the practice from a theoretical perspective, all definitions of residencies include the two concepts of time and space; although many other aspects in terms of the residency field are debatable, the problem of time and space will always remain central.

In this essay, I will present a more complex analysis of the historical and ideological implications of the practice of artist residencies. As in Sharon P. Holland's ground-breaking work, I will use her approximation to the historical problem of the face-to-face encounter, which includes acknowledging Frantz Fanon's observation in the time/space continuum, to understand the structural impediments and inequalities in the phenomenological readings of time and space in the context of residencies. In that regard, I will introduce what Holland refers to as the persistent problem of 'past' as 'place', that especially residencies in the Global South have to confront on a daily basis. What happens when an artist engages with artistic processes while immersed in a community where its culture, people, and even the place itself have been imagined and re-imagined by art history and, in general, the dominant visual culture? How can residencies become an affront to 'the order of things' and seize the opportunity to interrupt the violent continuity of history?

I will depart from Arquetopia's mission by beginning with a brief context on the historical development of the model of artist residencies as a result of the expansion of European empires. I will then elaborate on how Arquetopia's sustainable model has guaranteed its steady growth to become a transcontinental foundation and residency programme, allowing autonomy while enforcing ethical responsibility, especially considering the problematic relations between art and power. With the understanding of residencies as spaces where important ethical questions intersect, I will especially elaborate on Arquetopia's ethical commitment to approaching international encounters as opportunities for historical and ideological interruptions by introducing Emmanuel Levinas' ethics as the core of its methodology.

Arquetopia in the Context of Artist Residencies

Arquetopia was established in Puebla, Mexico, in 2009, as a small foundation with the mission of promoting development and social transformation through artistic, educational, and cultural programmes. Although development is rooted in the continental philosophy's ideals of 'freedom' and 'opportunities' to improve the well-being of individuals,[1] Arquetopia's model eventually would depart from this tradition to find a more suitable and unique model based on the interruption of these narratives of 'progress'. A permanent tension arose between the social scope of Arquetopia's mission, the legacy and discipline of art and art history, and the everyday face-to-face encounters, as it is not possible to address social transformation without recognizing the problematic relationship that art has with the structures of power.

To understand Arquetopia's model, it is necessary to contextualize the importance and historical development of residency programmes in general. Although residency programmes became a model that began to expand and multiply during the nineteenth and twentieth century, their historical roots can be traced to the French Academy in Rome in 1666 and the fellowships established in 1680 by the Real Academia de Bellas Artes de San Fernando (The Royal Academy of Fine Arts of San Fernando), which later became the Royal Academy of Spain in Rome (Hütter s.f.). The purpose of these institutions was to enable European artists to travel to Italy to improve their artistic training and stimulate their production under the auspices of the monarch.

By the nineteenth century, several nations around the world had established similar models. From Mexico, artists travelled to Europe on the Grand Tour with the sponsorship of the Academia Nacional de San Carlos (The National Academy of San Carlos); from the United States through the American Academy in Rome; and German artists were supported by the 'Prix de Rome' and the Prussian Academy of Arts (Guevara and Ortega 2013). Through official sponsorship, national regulation, and state protection, the relationship between artistic production and the exercise of imperial power became evident, and it was clear that ideology through artistic production was fundamental for the construction and consolidation of the Nation-State rhetoric. Also, during the 1800s, universal expositions originated, the international art biennial archetype was born, and national pavilions became the ultimate representation of national identity constructed through the language of art (Majluf 1997); however, it was not until the end of the nineteenth century that the term 'artist-in-residence' was coined. With the increasing support of patrons, the sponsorship of private collectors, and the goal of stimulating their artistic production, artists were frequently invited to *palazzos* and *villas*. As a result, they began to intervene in politics in a wider sense and from the private sphere, contributing to the construction of the national rhetoric. The course of art seemed to have suddenly changed in a revolutionary fashion; however, private interests have had a long-term involvement in this process, increasing the role of private collections in the public sphere and helping the emergence of criticism, art critics, and art publishing, ultimately fostering new modes of cultural production, national narratives included (Mancini 2005).

By the twentieth century, different models of academies, retreats, communes, and artists colonies had already been established in different parts of the world, though it was during the post-WWII decades that new types of residences aspiring to a utopia began to emerge, including the isolation or social participation of artists. Nevertheless, cultural globalization marked the point where residency programmes proliferated on a large scale—extending and intensifying social relations—and by the nineties, the increasing access to international travelling contributed to the development of many residency models with a very wide variety of cultural spaces. Despite this rapid growth, it was not until the twenty-first century that artist residency programmes became central to the global art production system, essential not only for the production of art but also for the dissemination of ideas on a global scale. Terry Smith, in her article 'Biennials and Infrastructural Shift—Part II', mentions that as of 2000, art biennials were faced with crises from overproduction, having become stale both in their exhibition formats and artistic content (Smith 2012). Meanwhile, at a local level, artist residencies gained so much traction that they became key infrastructure, even substituting government functions, having a flexible model effectively adapting to the local artistic and cultural needs, while impacting the development of artistic discourses at a global scale. It is in this context that Arquetopia emerges as a response to the complex state of the world, affecting local realities in Puebla and Oaxaca in Mexico, and Cusco in Peru.

Arquetopia and the Legacy of Art History in Latin America

The financial crisis of 2008, the strengthening of international borders, and especially the increasing levels of hate and violence in the United States, which directly affected my partner Christopher Davis' experience and my own, were catalysts that made us decide to establish Arquetopia, in 2009. Together with a small group of committed entrepreneurs and cultural practitioners, a clear vision, and a broad mission of promoting development and social transformation through the arts, we established the foundation in Puebla, Southern Mexico. Arquetopia began literally as an independent and alternative project in relation to the art structures of Mexico, gradually changing its position to become a reference in the residency field. Arquetopia became known for approaching art making with more rigorous practices, art history with critical perspectives, and acknowledging Mexico's and Peru's complexity in context by incorporating nuances in narratives and complex interpretation of visual culture.

The foundation began with an educational model that set the tone for the scope of its mission right from the start. It began as a programme for youth that, together with guest artists, explored various social issues, perspectives, and artistic approaches, with the goal of contributing to social change. Arquetopia's first few projects became the basis to what is now its core, the artist-in-residence programme with several branches, and specialties all rooted in different sources of knowledge or epistemologies. Some examples are the diverse textile arts of Mexico and Peru, which opened the door to understand the intricate local social fabric, not only as a repository of knowledge, arts, and daily practices, but as a structure of social obligations and material exchanges, including forms of reciprocity such as bartering. These complex structures of social obligations are an alternative mode of collective redistribution and resource development that is not confined to material wealth, but includes symbolic and social wealth, which altogether expands the commons and guarantees subsistence to communities. Although artist residencies are created under the premise of cultural exchanges, not all forms of exchanges are just; reciprocity, however, premises on negotiations that develop social capital, weave cultural fabrics, and expand resources for present and future use.

The foundation's cornerstone is sustainable development through four main principles embodied in all of Arquetopia's programmes and activities: social awareness, shared responsibility, innovation, and local networks development. This has entailed a process of continuous revision of its model and the implementation of dynamic language in all procedures, activities, and discussions. This constant revision is also aimed at revealing the historical systems of exploitation as a legacy of modernity,[2] allowing the renegotiation of terms of interactions between participants, especially in the process of face-to-face encounters, and the content in the forms of communication, which directly impact the production of art.

As a result, and after almost ten years in the residency field, Arquetopia has become a space where many realities and complexities converge. Every year, Arquetopia's artist-in-residence programmes offer professional opportunities for emerging and established artists, both national and foreign. Arquetopia's mission has been inclusive right from the beginning, and its residency has become a culturally diverse space with a multiplicity of perspectives, by hosting every year artists, scholars, researchers, and professionals of the arts, from different ages, gender identities, and very diverse cultures, from more than 75 countries spanning all regions of the world. Its aim is to encourage the critical dialogue about North/South agendas, challenge global curatorial biases, and address contradictions between market forces and artistic independence. This implies bringing a high level of complexity and worldwide social tensions, as well as preconceptions about Mexico and Peru–many of them, in fact, rooted in art and art history–into a limited and specific physical space, which reflects on the relationships that artists-in-residence establish with each other and the local communities. As Donald Preziosi states, art history is deeply invested in the continuous fabrication of modernity, making the very idea of 'art' seem natural and an innate 'universal' phenomenon.

> From a Eurocentric point of view, art history appears to be a universal science, systematically discovering and explicating specimens of a seemingly universal human phenomenon–'art'–the 'art' of all peoples, all arranged relative to

> each other as at a universal exposition, with each allotted its proper historical and geographical space: representatives in a congress of equals (Preziosi 1999).

Nevertheless, the construction of the visual history of Latin America is much more complex. Since the first encounters between Europeans and the inhabitants of the Americas, the production of images about *Mesoamerica*[3] and the Andes, up to modern day Mexico and Peru (as well as many other regions in the Global South[4]) were the result of descriptions through the imperial European gaze. For instance, the first narration of the encounter with Moctezuma II was made by Spaniards, which then was translated into other European languages in the form of text, and later became images through engravings. Most of the illustrators and artists who produced images about the Americas never set foot on either continent; however, many of their images were sent to the Viceroyalties of the New Spain (Mexico) and Peru, to teach and train local artists. Subsequently these images were used to create paintings, the artistic expression of imperial power par excellence. Such gazes and forms of interpretation continue to be the visual references for all of Latin America, establishing the parameters of a visual culture that would linger for over 500 years. Even now, one of the beer labels in Mexico carrying the name of Moctezuma continues to be visually rooted in the historical descriptions, categorizations, and gaze that Europeans exercised in the process of the invasion of the Americas. This is especially relevant as we learn that we have very limited agency over the visual culture surrounding us, and that this has been articulated with the goal of categorizing and the intention of dominating through visual control (Preziosi 1999). These methods permeate all forms of visual representation of nature, the objects around us as well as people, establishing gender roles, social classes, racial categories, and forms of social and cultural organization. The visual culture of the Americas through religious images, colonial portraits, still life, and landscape, as well as maps, engravings, and book illustrations generated a complex visual tradition that paradoxically contributed to the development of Mexico as a nation and also coined the perception of an exotic paradise, very different and very far away from the European 'order' (Katzew 2004). This is how a paradigm was created, a historical system of exploitation that observes, imagines, and describes the culture and inhabitants of all of Latin America, linking them to adjectives such as 'tradition', 'magic', 'picturesque', and 'colourful', always oppositional to 'progress', 'technology', 'development', and 'modernity' to name a few.

These ways of imagining and describing Latin America are of great relevance to everyday life, as they govern perceptions of reality and affect individual experiences especially in the way foreigners perceive these regions. These perceptions are particularly relevant to residency programmes, since residencies host artists who inevitably with their gazes, participate in imagining, describing, and engaging others through the process of art making (Nochlin 1983). For these reasons, there is an ethical responsibility inherent to the practice of artist residencies, especially considering the diversity of local communities that get involved and the disparity of power relations that arise from many of their interactions. I will further explore this by presenting Sharon P. Holland's concepts regarding the one-on-one encounter, oppositional binaries, and the problem of 'past' as 'place'.

Face-to-Face Encounters at Arquetopia

I have presented artist residencies as spaces where ideologies, ontological questions, philosophy, and anthropological theories converge through the many encounters taking place there. Also, the Levinasian concept of 'Other' (which I will later fully explain) becomes relevant to these meetings. Precisely, Levinas articulates that the preeminent reason for engaging in an encounter is the Other's difference, which all of us desire to understand (Levinas 1991). Considering the complexity of differences that artist residencies engage with, I will address the time/space continuum in the transcendental problem of the face-to-face encounter through my experience at Arquetopia, while expanding on the implications of such intersection happening in the context of Puebla, Oaxaca, and Cusco, and the negotiations of the processes of differentiation occurring through the artist-in-residence programmes.

In an encounter, several processes of differentiation and negotiation occur, re-enacting complex historical relationships of superiority and inferiority in relation to different scales and contexts. As Sharon P. Holland states, in her book *The Erotic Life of Racism*, too often, in the encounter, we want to read the present as if it were living in the past; we cast a shadow over the interpretative work that we perform, not even knowing that this meeting has already been scripted (Holland 2012). In that sense, we actively construct and enact a binary relation that articulates differences in opposition to our very existence, making assumptions from an unfounded perspective of privilege. Such binaries are established through concepts that create separation, dissimilarity, distinction, and inferiority; ultimately defining the relation as 'those who shape time' and 'those who stand outside it', those who belong to your people and those who do not. There are many examples in history, such as Male vs. Female, West vs. East, Europeans vs. Indigenous, White vs. Black, and the seeming tension between these two 'opposites' continuously impact the perceptions of ethnicity, social class, and gender, among many others, in the process of a face-to-face encounter.

For instance, in his book *Black Skin, White Masks* (p. 218), Frantz Fanon reflects on the time/space continuum:

> When it encounters resistance from the other, self-consciousness undergoes the experience of desire... As soon as I desire I ask to be considered. I am not merely here and now, sealed into thingness. I am for somewhere else and for something else. I demand that notice be taken of my negating activity–in so far as I pursue something other than life ...
>
> I occupied space. I moved towards the other... and the evanescent other, hostile but not opaque, transparent, not there, disappeared. Nausea.

Holland expands on this notion by presenting the ideological problem of 'past' as 'place', as being locked in a past that becomes a tremendous burden to the present. For instance, what happens when someone who exists in time seeks to meet someone who only occupies space? Those who seem to control time, order the world and represent the industry of progressiveness, however those animals and humans who seem to have no world-making effect only occupy space and appear as the antithesis of history; thus, the crossing seems impossible and almost never happens (Holland 2012). Holland continues to explain that when a binary intersects in space, 'the outer limit of doing and being are exercised and felt by those who have to negotiate their place [in the encounter]'. She argues that although inequalities that emerge from encounters are often talked about, the phenomenological reading of time and space is rarely addressed to understand structural impediments and inequalities. For instance, artists-in-residence are engaging, with biological and cultural differences as part of the process of the encounters on a daily basis; however, these facts are secondary to the meeting itself and the meaning attributed to them. In that sense, as we acknowledge the discipline and legacy of art and art history in the context of residencies, this is precisely why most foreign artists would imagine and see a local artist or residency manager as mired in space, while in contrast, they would imagine themselves as representing the full expanse of time. As a result, the encounter might be thought of as never occurring in the same temporal plane. Then again, encounters are never static, and in the negotiating process of the meeting a resistance to the binary may manifest itself on either side, which speaks about a sense of time and space beyond historical constraints, challenging every notion of the Other.

It is precisely Emmanuel Levinas, the preeminent twentieth-century philosopher of ethics, who addresses this resistance by shifting the focus on the experience of the 'I'[5] to an emphasis on the Other (*Autrui*).[6] In his book *Meaning and Sense*, Levinas asks, 'Is the Desire for the Other an appetite or a generosity?' (Levinas 1987), thereby questioning the means rather than the ends of such engagement. Through his work, he was very concerned with the epistemological and ontological privilege assigned to the rational self (I) that exaggerates its potential of knowing and defining, ethically violating everything (besides the self) and forcing it into a mould suitable to its own ontology. Departing from protecting the Other from this ontological violence, Levinas prioritizes its alterity over the repressive self and its metaphysical machinations. This is how he radically redefines the Other as a priority, as a transcendent presence that cannot be contained or eclipsed by the totality of experience of the I (Bolton 2010). In contrast with continental philosophy, this Other has an infinite transcendence and is unnameable, undefinable, and uncontrollable. In fact, the only way to contact the Other is for it to intrude in the world of the I and rock its perceptions with a commanding face asserting the need to respect the integrity of differences, differences which validate –not negate– his/her existence in the world (Holland 2012). Audre Lorde, in her famous text *The Master's Tools Will Never Dismantle the Master's House*, states that non-dominant differences are the raw powerful interconnection from which our personal power is created, and this interdependency enables knowledge and the concomitant power to provoke change (Lorde 1984).

One of the fundamental principles of Levinasian ethics is the criticism of the privilege of freedom as a value in which sacrifice and oppression are needed, thus disproving the classical relationship between the 'I'[7] and the 'Other' (Peperzak 2003). Emmanuel Levinas also radically changes the traditional concept of the subject as the 'I' and qualifies it as a being who never stays the same. He proposes that the 'I' existence does not consist of its identity, but is a dynamic, continuous process of identification, meaning the integration of its identity through everything that happens in every moment (Bolton 2010). This concept is radically different from the idea that the identity of a being is something static, by considering a constant performativity[8] (a process of performance, representation, interpretation, and realization) of that being in the context of others. Levinas proposes that the encounter is the essence of ethics and states 'the relationship with the Other puts me into question, empties me of myself and empties me without end, showing me ever new resources' (Levinas 1996).

These concepts are of great significance to explain the process of any face-to-face encounter, but especially in the context of an artist residency. They enable us to explain the desire of artists to seek artist residencies as facilitators for meetings and encounters, but they also help elucidate the controlling gaze that accompanies most forms of art production. Knowing this, Arquetopia contests the controlling gaze, which wants to define and categorize, by recognizing in the encounter a greater responsibility and the possibility of justice.

Over the years, Arquetopia has developed a series of methodologies founded on Levinasian ethics and local epistemologies, making face-to-face encounters more complex, artistic practices more responsible, and prioritizing the development of horizontal collaborations, and reciprocal exchanges (Guevara 2016). Arquetopia's programmes identify knowledge to stimulate local development and long-term social change by taking every opportunity to assertively negotiate the reinvestment of resources into learning and exchange opportunities to address larger issues in contemporary societies. With a goal to promote synergy and collaboration, Arquetopia considers innovation, feasibility, reciprocity, and respect for local knowledge indispensable factors for the creative process. All of the foundation's programmes are based on a non-exploitative model promoting social consciousness, and artists-in-residence are strongly encouraged to explore various ways of cultural exchange as part of their artistic and/or research goals and to actively engage in critical discussions as part of their residency experience (Guevara 2009).

The foundation's methodology encompasses a process of revealing the ideological complexities of making art by presenting a multifaceted context and emphasizing a self-reflective, critical thought process for all the participants. Each project renegotiates relations of power by examining artistic purpose, context, performativity of participants (both local and foreign), as well as history, culture, and politics, to reveal misconceptions of the sense of time and space in the forms of representation used by the artist. In order to accomplish its mission, Arquetopia has developed a North-South interchange through residencies that focus on identifying conflict in the creative and exchange processes. In collaboration with Arquetopia's staff, Kirsten Buick, art historian and member of the board of directors, has significantly contributed to the development of tools, including the articulation of a necessary dynamic language, allowing us to rethink the relationship between art, privilege, and power structures. The foundation's methodology considers the artist's gaze a departing point that–through the performativity of race, class, and gender, among other aspects–creates a problem in the realm of art history. For instance, many artists come to Mexico and Peru seeking for the 'authentic', and in some form or other they engage with visual exploitation through their artistic practice. Examples of terms that create the ideological problem of time as place, are ones that I have previously mentioned and often included in residency project descriptions, such as: 'picturesque', 'colourful', 'magical', 'traditional', 'indigeneity', and even 'authentic'. We have to acknowledge that Latin America, and especially Mexico and Peru, has been the object of imperialist fantasies since the invasion of Hernán Cortés in the sixteenth century (Cummins 2002). Since then, the Americas and its inhabitants have been imagined and re-imagined in opposition to colonizers. For example, America and cannibals are almost simultaneous European inventions, and all the descriptions of Mesoamerica and the Andes over the following centuries were tied to discourses of idolatry and cannibalism, making a distinction between self and other, and especially between history and place (Cummins 2002). Following that trajectory, 'picturesque' emerged in the eighteenth century, creating a point of view that frames the world, turning nature into a series of living *tableaux* (Marshall 2002). Mexico was no exception, and in the period following its independence, Anglo imagination invented the idea of Mexican landscape through diaries of travellers and explorers (Braham 2008). In that sense, the very idea of landscape implies separation and observation, and any description of an art project intending to use landscape in the context of Mexico or Peru is very problematic. As Kirsten Buick states, landscape erases as much as it reveals; landscape representation in the Americas is inherently an eraser of the native population's extermination and the exploitation of African labour, therefore landscape and empire are automatically implicated (Cash and Rojas 2016).

In many ways, Arquetopia serves as a mediator, interlocutor, facilitator, and curator by strategically bringing together international artists with local artists, youth, as well as cultural producers to facilitate knowledge exchange, mobilize resources, and expand spaces for dialogue and dissemination. Its methodologies emphasize education about power, promoting dialogue, analyzing critically artistic approaches, and expanding the spaces where art is formalized. Over the years, the Foundation has developed strong working relationships through cross-pollination and trust building with a wide range of local artists, as well as art and educational institutions both in Mexico and Peru. By focusing on the face-to-face encounter, Arquetopia facilitates a meticulous negotiation to alter historical relations of power. As a result, Northern-based artists exchange skills and knowledge with local artists, art studios, and museums, gaining insights and experiences while making art in diverse and stimulating cultural environments. The local arts communities benefit from this exchange by increasing their resources, while also experimenting and learning. Participants are empowered through social awareness, recognition of local knowledge, and systematization of artistic practices. In this process, the epistemological origin is also shifted, and Arquetopia refocuses artist-in-residence projects to challenge notions of authenticity articulated through the idea of 'tradition' by contrasting them with the concept of knowledge and therefore contesting the problem of past as place.

To illustrate, local artists are invited as instructors and teach artists-in-residence a specific knowledge or technology that Arquetopia has previously identified as important to the culture of Puebla, Oaxaca, or Cusco. In the process, instructors have complete freedom not only to decide the content and method for the classes, but also to teach in their own language, which shifts the epistemological origin in the exchange, and refocuses the process on the one-on-one encounter. In other words, for the exchange to happen they need to acknowledge each other and renegotiate the rules for communication, allowing differences and subtleties to emerge in the interpretation, forcing them to recognize in the encounter a much more dynamic and contingent process. Additionally, young students from local universities and schools benefit through their participation in the different programmes by learning and developing skills, organizing activities, documenting the processes, and facilitating exchanges. It's precisely at this juncture where the integrity of differences as sine qua non for encounters becomes an ethical transcendent experience.

Conclusion

Face-to-face encounters are reminders of our own existence and the intersubjective relations encompassing our experience. In that sense, artist residencies have a preeminent role, not only in the art ecosystems but also as facilitators of encounters by providing time, space, and resources between diverse communities and multiple individuals, and art. In such a model, being called by another and responding to that other is implicit, and a fundamental, powerful experience in which ethics is to be discovered. At Arquetopia, every residency is an opportunity to ignite change, challenge the sense of time and space, and approach art practices with ethical responsibility. Over the years, Arquetopia's structure has functioned as a regulating space where forms of artistic production are firmly renegotiated and where the resources gained are reinvested to make local development possible. Arquetopia's artist-in-residence programmes have become a reference in the worldwide art ecosystem with a model that challenges 'the order of things' based on non-exploitative practices that actively engage partners, communities, and artists-in-residence in various ways of reciprocal exchanges. In that sense, knowledge has been a key resource to stimulate local development and promote social change on a long-term basis. Face-to-face encounters will continue to ask questions about justice, goodness, and ethics; this is how, for the last ten years, Arquetopia has been invested in respecting the integrity of differences, with the expectation that such concerns will once again be relevant in artistic practices in general.

Notes

1 A United Nations Development Program introduced in 1990, the first Human Development Report with a new approach for advancing human wellbeing. Human development–or the human development approach–is about expanding the richness of human life, rather than simply the richness of the economy in which human beings live. It is an approach that is focused on people and their opportunities and choices.

2 Ramón Grosfoguel in his essay 'The Structure of Knowledge in Westernized Universities' uses the term *Modernity* to explain the new historical system known as the Capitalist World-Economy. He also uses this term to explain how the 'West' kidnapped and monopolized the definition of Democracy, Human Rights, Women liberation, Economy, etc.

3 *Mesoamerica* is the historical and cultural region in the America that includes Mexico and Central America in which pre-Hispanic societies flourished before the European invasion of the Americas in the fifteenth and sixteenth century.

4 *Global South* is a term emerging from transnational and postcolonial studies to include regions and countries that share common histories of colonization, and imperialism, confronting large inequalities.

5 In 1961 *Totalité et Infini: essai sur l'extériorité* (Totality and Infinity) appeared, in which Levinas consolidated his philosophical originality. Within the first few pages, Levinas defines Continental philosophy as an 'Ego', or an 'I', whose integrity of being is founded on the individual sense of oneself as an identity; having a sole source of its own essence, without considering anything external for its constitution.

6 *Autrui* refers only to a human other or others, has no plural but refers to a plural referent, and can also be employed as a reverential or intimate mode of address, as 'you'. Moreover, it permits no definite or indefinite article, and cannot be made an epithet. Derrida first noted these issues in considering Levinas, and explained that *autrui* is 'in its sense, indeclinable and outside genre', and 'does not designate a species of the genre autre' (Galetti 2015).

7 Levinas challenges European philosophy by providing an argument that displaces the assumption about the primacy of self-willed agency in the study of ethics, by presenting an alternative responsiveness to the Other. The 'I' find its identity in response to the Other, as a result the 'I' or self emerges as a by-product, a responsive derivative construction.

8 Performativity refers to the process of continuous building of identities, which implies that these can be open, multiple, or even contradictory. This identification process has an emphasis on procedural qualities and is carried out through signification practices subject to positional and relational social locations. For Victor Turner performance has the capacity to reveal classifications, categories, and contradictions of the forms of social organization of a group and its relationships of power and hierarchy.

Literature

- Baldwin, James. *The Price of the Ticket: Collected Nonfiction, 1948-1985*. New York: St. Martin's/Marek, 1985.
- Baudez, Claude-François. 'History of Art and Anthropology of Art.' *RES: Anthropology and Aesthetics* 42 (Autumn 2002), pp. 139-41. Available at www.jstor.org/stable/20167574.
- Bolton, Linda. *Facing the Other: Ethical Disruption and the American Mind (Horizons in Theory and American Culture).* Louisiana: Louisiana State University Press, 2010.
- Braham, Persephone. 'Adventures in the Picturesque: Voyage and Voyeurism in the Tourist Guidebook to Mexico.' *Revista Canadiense De Estudios Hispánicos* 26, no. 3 (2002), pp. 379-94. Available at www.jstor.org/stable/27763778.
- Cash, Stephanie, and Carl Rojas. 'Q&A with Kirsten Pai Buick.' *BURNAWAY*, 18 March 2016. Available at burnaway.org/interview/kirsten-pai-buick/, accessed 18 August 2018.
- Cormier, Ray. 'Travel Advisory: Woodstock: Art Colony Tells Its Story.' *New York Times*, 29 June 2003. Available at www.nytimes.com/2003/06/29/travel/travel-advisory-woodstock-art-colony-tells-its-story.html, accessed 3 March 2018.
- Cosgrove, Denis. 'Prospect, Perspective and the Evolution of the Landscape Idea.' *Transactions of the Institute of British Geographers* 10, no. 1 (1985), pp. 45-62. doi:10.2307/622249.
- Cummins, Thomas. 'To Serve Man: Pre-Columbian Art, Western Discourses of Idolatry, and Cannibalism.' *RES: Anthropology and Aesthetics* 42 (2002), pp. 109-30. Available at www.jstor.org/stable/20167572.
- Fanon, Frantz. *Black Skin, White Masks*. New York: Grove Press, 1967. Originally published as *Peau noir, masques blanc*. Paris: Éditions de Seuil, 1952.
- Galetti, Dino 'The grammar of Levinas' other, Other, *autrui, Autrui*: Addressing translation Conventions and Interpretation in English-language Levinas Studies.' *South African Journal of Philosophy* 34, no. 2 (April 2015), pp 199-213.
- Grosfoguel, Ramón. 'A TimeSpace Perspective on Development: Recasting Latin American Debates.' *Review (Fernand Braudel Center)* 20, no. 3-4 (1997), pp. 465-540. Available at www.jstor.org/stable/40241411.

  –. 'The Structure of Knowledge in Westernized Universities: Epistemic Racism/Sexism and the Four Genocides/Epistemicides of the Long 16th Century.' *Human Architecture: Journal of the Sociology of Self-Knowledge* XI (Fall 2013), pp. 73-90.
- Guevara, Francisco. 'Our Mission.' 2 July 2009. Available at www.arquetopia.org/about-us/our-mission, accessed 8 April 2018.

  –. 'Arquetopia Foundation & International Artist Residency: Arquetopia Foundation and International Artist Residency.' Available at www.arquetopia.org/, accessed 2016.

  –, & E. Ortega. '¿Criollo yo?: Residuos post-coloniales en la gestión de la cultura en México.' *Magazyn Sztuki* 4 (2013), pp. 49-57.
- Holland, Sharon P. *The Erotic Life of Racism*. Duke University Press. Kindle Edition, 2012.
- Human Development Reports. 'Human Development Reports.' 2014. Available at hdr.undp.org/en/humandev.
- Hütter, Verena. 'Residencies: History of the Artists Villas.' Available at www.goethe.de/ges/prj/res/mag/por/en9519580.htm, accesed 30 June 2016.
- Jones, Amelia, and Andrew Stephenson. *Performing the Body: Performing the Text.* New York: Routledge, 1999.
- Katzew, Ilona. *Casta Paintings: Images of Race in Eighteenth-Century Mexico.* Singapore: Yale University Press, 2004.
- Lorde, Audre. 'The Master's Tools Will Never Dismantle the Master's House.' In *Sister Outsider: Essays and Speeches*, pp. 110-14. Berkeley, CA: Crossing Press, 1984.
- Levinas, Emmanuel. 'Meaning and Sense.' In *Collected Philosophical Papers. Phaenomenologica* (Collection Fondée par H.L. van Breda et Publiée sous le Patronage des Centres d'Archives-Husserl), vol. 100. Dordrecht: Springer, 1987.

  –. *Totality and Infinity: An Essay on Exteriority.* The Hague: Kluwer Academic Publishers, 1991.
- Lomnitz, Claudio. *Deep Mexico, Silent*

Mexico: An Anthropology of Nationalism. Minneapolis: University of Minnesota Press, 2001.
— Majluf, Natalia. '"Ce n'est pas le Pérou," or, the Failure of Authenticity: Marginal Cosmopolitans at the Paris Universal Exhibition of 1855.' *Critical Inquiry* 23, no. 4 (1997), pp. 868-93. Available at www.jstor.org/stable/1344052.
— Mancini, JoAnne Marie. *Pre-Modernism: Art World Change and American Culture from the Civil War to the Armory Show*. New Jersey: Princeton University Press, 2005.
— Marshall, David. 'The Problem of the Picturesque.' *Eighteenth-Century Studies* 35, no. (2002), pp. 413-37. Available at www.jstor.org/stable/30054207.
— Moyer, Harley. *The Priority of the Human in the Philosophy of Emmanuel Levinas*. (Unpublished Master's thesis). Oregon: University of Oregon, 2010.
— Nochlin, Linda. *The Politics of Vision: Essays on Nineteenth-Century Art and Society*. New York: Routledge, 1989.
— Phillips, Ruth B., and Christopher B. Steiner. *Unpacking Culture: Art and Commodity in Colonial and Postcolonial Worlds*. Berkeley and Los Angeles: University of California Press, 1999.
— Peperzak, Adriaan. 'Ethical Life.' *Research in Phenomenology* 33 (2003), pp. 141-54. Available at www.jstor.org/stable/24660613.
— Pinder, Kymberly N. *Race-ing Art History: Critical Readings in Race and Art*. New York: Routledge, 2002.
— Preziosi, Donald. 'Virtual (Art) History.' *RACAR: Revue D'art Canadienne/Canadian Art Review* 26, no. 1-2 (1999), pp. 91-95. Available at www.jstor.org/stable/42630613.
— Purbrick, Louise. 'Cloth, Gender, Politics: The Armagh Handkerchief, 1976.' *Clio (English Edition)* 40 (2014), pp. 105-23. Available at www.jstor.org/stable/26238764.
— Real Academia de España en Roma. 'Desde 1873 hasta hoy: Presencia Española en Roma.' 2016. Available at www.accademiaspagna.org/historia/, accessed 1 February 2018.
— Res Artis. 'Definition of Artist Residencies.' Available at www.resartis.org/en/residencies/about_residencies/definition_of_artist_residencies/, accessed 30 May 2018.
— Res Artis. 'Vision, Mission & Values.' Available at www.resartis.org/en/about/about_res_artis/vision_mission__values/, accessed 20 July 2016.
— Schama, Simon. *The Power of Art*. New York: Ecco, 2006.
— Smith, Terry. 'Biennials and Infrastructural Shift - Part II.' ArtAsiaPacific 80 (2012).
— Stanford Encyclopedia of Philosophy. 'Emmanuel Levinas.' Available at 30 May 2018, from https://plato.stanford.edu/entries/levinas/.
— Turner, Victor W. *The Anthropology of Performance*. New York: PAJ Publications, 1988.

Rooted and Slow Institutions Reside in Remote Places

Vytautas Michelkevičius

What kind of elements constitute a remote residency and its poetics? Location, season, inner and outer community, staff, rituals, mission and visions, local intellectuals, heritage, connectedness to local, regional, global scenes. What about time and its qualities such as speed, pace, and seasonality? We should also include in the list the way of travel and difficult accessibility. And then it becomes even more unclear why artists from comfortable urbanized metropolises fly or go by boat or ground transport thousands of kilometres to remote and secluded locations all around the world.

The concept of remote art institutions has existed since the twenties and thirties (for example: Black Mountain College[1]) but it has only properly arrived in the public and commercial art markets and become an important part of their infrastructures in recent decades. Because of the decentralization of former metropolises known as art centres, ubiquitous communication technologies and their increasing power, and the rural turning into post-rural,[2] remote places lost their disadvantages and became as central or connected as everything everywhere.

This is a practice-based reflection on eight years co-running a residency in a small resort village on the coast of the Baltic Sea in Lithuania, situated between Nordic and Central-Eastern Europe or, to put in postcolonial terms–not-yet-recognized and debatable 'Global East'. The text also includes experiences from numerous visits to other remote residency places around Europe and a few in China and Brazil.

Despite my background in academic research (with PhD and postdoc in humanities and social sciences), this text is mostly based on practice-based research and insights which came during my curatorial and artistic directorship while running artists-in-residency, education and art centre–Nida Art Colony. It is a non-profit state-funded institution, providing free education and public art programmes. It is also one of the largest art universities in the Nordic-Baltic region.

The residency model of Nida Art Colony is quite unique. It is affiliated to the Vilnius Academy of Arts, which is a university with BA, MA, PhD and DA programmes in visual art, applied art, design, architecture, art history & theory, culture management, and politics. It functions in three parallel and inter-related courses: international residency programme (at least five residents at a time), education centre hosting student workshops and organizing Nida Doctoral School, and contemporary art producer with exhibitions, publications, and production of two Lithuanian Pavilions in the Venice Biennale (2015 and 2019). The remoteness of Nida Art Colony is defined by travel time (five hours to the capital Vilnius and the academy's headquarters), geographical isolation (the last leg includes a ferry and drive down 50 kilometres across the Curonian Spit) and geopolitical situation (two kilometres to the Russian border, which is also the border with the European Union).

I have been working here since the late 2010s, before the reconstruction of the venue was finished and it was officially launched in March 2011. Among other things, I was involved in other residency visits, active participation (and initiation) in regional and international networks, how-to seminars, conferences, curatorial residencies, almost one hundred open studios, residency launching events, and giving advice to cultural administrative units and councils. All this, of course, rendered many insights into the residencies but also probably raised many more questions than answers, and it is these questions that I want to raise and discuss in this essay.

SLOWNESS: Travel, Time, and Research

The pace of an institution is often constituted by its location. Most of the time, the artist-in-residency in a metropolis will be hectic, whereas in a rural location it will be slow and sometimes relaxing. However, 'slow' does not mean lazy or lethargic. It is a deliberate slowness and removal from various pressures in everyday schedules. Sometimes in this kind of programmes you have only one formal meeting with a curator or director to exchange the experiences and there is even no need to mention the final result or outcome of the residency. It might come in a month or two, or even sometimes in several years.

Traveling to a Place

Travel to and from a remote residency is always an important experience included in the residency itself. Without long and exhausting physical travel, you will not realize the level of remoteness of the place. Moreover, the last leg of the trip is usually exceptional, weird, and difficult, as if to emphasize the inaccessibility of the place. You need to take a ferry (Nida Art Colony), be transported by a boat to the island (Røst AiR, Lofoten Islands, Norway), have a personal pick up by car or 4x4 Jeep, ride on a camel, pass the steep slope down to the fjord, which might be closed during snowstorms (Skaftfell Center for Visual Art, Iceland), join a scientist community with a special flight (residencies in Antarctic research stations), or even walk for a few kilometres on foot. This last leg usually involves a conceptual detachment from your everyday life and makes you dependent on locals, staff, or special access to the required vehicles. Since artists become more and more sensitive to CO_2 footprint, they choose ground or sea transport instead of flights. In this case the trip becomes a journey and this physical experience strengthens the dimension of time and the distance of the final destination because sometimes it takes several days to reach it from your home. Slow travel starts the experience of the slow residency and brings the resident into the right track. Not to forget that the landscape you experience through the travel window is being slowly transformed from the one you know to that of the prospective one. The slow speed of travel facilitates the shift both in your mind and body and gives you time to leave your needless ideas behind and prepare for new ones. Like a custom with some African tribes urges you to sit down for a while after a long trip by bus and allow your soul to catch up with you after fast travel.

Therefore, in the age of the virtual, travelling to remote places intensifies the physicality of the everyday and the longing for bodily experience, which also influences the mind and way of working. Despite the growing number of virtual residencies, the residency attached to a specific place that offers complete immersion into the environment and is able to secure a productive or retreat-like space, is still in great demand and use by artists, curators, writers, and other creative practitioners.

Rest, Retreat, Respite, Decelerate... Research

In the culture of wellness and mindfulness spas, residencies play an important role in accommodating artists and their needs. The slow pace of the location is also transferred to the residency and every morning residents start thinking it is Sunday again. The urge to answer urgent emails is reduced to a minimum and this is probably because of the physical remoteness from your job obligations, commissionaires, producers, gallerists, dealers, curators, and critics.

Biological rhythms change drastically as well. Residents start sleeping longer or sometimes even suffer from insomnia.

Too much fresh air may either invite jogging or the desperation of physical inactivity.

To facilitate that kind of environment, the institution also has to take over the pace of the place and support the slowness of the process and production. In some cases, it is like a castle or monastery to escape the speed of contemporaneity. Remote locations are really beneficial places to help slow down time. When you go out into nature or a small town, you see that nothing happens, and the control of time is given back to you as an artist.

A residency should facilitate various qualities of slowness: working with no daily schedule, informal critique, home-cooked food, long conversations by the fire in summer and around hot pie and a tea pot in winter. In the end, slowness is an advantage and escape, which is a very important quality of most remote residencies. Among other advantages, a remote residency can provide an almost competition-free environment for artists and their peers, writers, curators, and other kind of creative practitioners. During the residency you have your peers together with local staff and visiting curators and in most cases they form a critical but friendly and cosy community for developing work and testing new ideas. The lack of urban aspects (a gang of art professionals and random visitors) and people who already think in stereotypes about your practice, enables remote residents to get onto the new track and develop new ideas or receive critique from new peers.

Relatively new programmes in artistic practice-based PhD can also sometimes be treated as long-term residency programmes, especially if they have funding. They secure for artists three to four years of protection from the commercial art market and provide a critical community to have freedom to develop artistic practices and produce new work as well as to participate in social dialogue.

Green Cube as Abolishment of White Cube

In most cases of remote residencies the concept of 'white cube' must be abandoned. It simply doesn't work, either because of the lack of audiences comfortable with white cube or because of other specific conditions of the local place, such as heritage architecture made of wood and bricks.

I have developed the concept of the 'green cube'[3] for the Nida Art Colony situation and it could be transposed to other residencies working in protected remote areas (like Banff residency in the National Park in Canada). Since decades, beautiful sceneries have been very tempting for artist to add something to it and call it 'Land Art'. It represents a very anthropocentric treatment of environment with a desire to insert something and make it more beautiful. But for whom?

However, due to the strict regulations limiting or even prohibiting human interventions, (National) nature parks become sanctuaries of nature. Therefore, both keepers/rangers and visitors treat them as museums where every piece of nature (a tree, a bush, a stone, a lichen) is a piece of (natural) art. One can only walk there and admire them. The whole park is like a green cube where only artefacts from its context can be inserted. For example, in the National Park of the Curonian Spit, forestation is constantly managed, and some trees are cut, some are replaced, new ones are planted. It is on the UNESCO world heritage list and protected from almost all human activity, including permanent artistic interventions. Therefore, the park is mostly used as a temporary but oversized studio or exhibition space, but the environment always has to be restored to the previous condition, as in any white cube.

Of course, greenness of the cube is more complicated than whiteness. First of all, it is constantly changing because plants are growing and responding to the seasons. For example, in one of the early Nida Art Colony projects, artist Justin Tyler Tate built a basketball playground from wooden Euro-pallets in a protected forest. In the beginning it was a very temporary installation, but the artist really wanted to give it to nature and see how the forest would take back the wood used for the pallets. The grasses were steeping through the cracks and splits, the floor was covered in pine needles and later in fallen leaves and started to rot. In the end, we managed to obtain permission for this installation to stay for the whole year to experience all the seasons. Therefore, it also got snow, ice and new green lush. During the change of the seasons it transformed from a functional playground into a sculpture. And the initial artist's idea to experience higher baskets as the trees grow was realized too. Luckily, the green cube is also resilient and after small interventions can restore itself.

Moreover, the National Park of the Curonian Spit is protected as a cultural landscape, which corresponds to the discourse of invented or constructed nature[4] and supports 'the park as a museum' concept. There is no need to pretend anymore that nature is not natural in the age of Anthropocene. This understanding should be increased and promoted–the nature in the park is invented and constructed with the power of human creativity. 'Wild' parks and variety of their habitats are designed for the sake of flora and fauna. But maybe first of all for human beings who either feel guilty about their previous activities as the superior species or simply want to enjoy the richness of nature–indeed this is a museum and the collections always have to be renewed and enlarged.

Another thing is the evergreen-ness of the local National Park because pine forests are nearly the same all year round and both moss and pines are a sort of green colour–only the light changes. If you come in February or August, May or November, it might be not easy to differentiate the seasons. Therefore, you can easily lose the sense of seasonality. In the end, this feeling enhances the green cube idea even more and provides stability to the artists during their work and leisure.

What could contemporary artists do there if they are not a follower of the representational tradition of historical artists' colonies where artists simply represented and communicated the beauty of nature? They suddenly become dislocated from their urban rhythms and studios to a very beautiful scenery, which sometimes becomes quite dangerous to their artistic practice, especially if they start treating it literally. If this is the case, many artists become trapped in the artefacts of nature and start collecting them (pine cones, driftwood, moss and lichen, and so on) and arranging them into something which they think looks like a not-yet-seen site-specific installation or original artistic research. Luckily, the representational relationship with nature in most cases is over in contemporary art but ready-made strategy is still very viable and dangerously helps artist lose their heads. But how can you submit to the sublime, when this stunning vastness of the open sea hides thousands of tons of human waste or reforested plateaus cover hundreds of years of human influence on primeval forests? The pressure of the Anthropocene strikes you time and again.

The artists who benefit most from the vastness of the green cube are often the ones who treat it more as a fitness room than as a gallery, with performative practices sometimes as a very nice exception. No, I do not mean only jogging or other workout-related activity but also Thalassotherapy–the systematic use of seawater, sea products, and shore climate. Swimming, hiking, and inhaling rich in iodide air makes artists more fit for their creative activities.

Not to forget climbing the different types of dunes and mountains and opening perspectives for your eyes and treating them with vast and scenic panoramas.

There is also a third strategy–to employ methods from traditional foraging, local knowledge, herbal medicine, scientific biology, cultural heritage, landscape architecture, marine, landscape, and nature parks management and develop your own project. So, in that case, because there is no urban information overload, artists dig into natural informational surroundings which after some research opens up piles of new knowledge and experience. Of course, in the initial stages they are new only for the artist but after longer development they manage to discover and expose something new for wider audiences or even for professional practitioners of these domains.

Therefore, artists become contributors and developers of the specific place and transgress the borders of art and artistic practice. They start changing local administrative practice and development of research-based scenarios of that specific remote place. Artists become policy makers and influencers, urban and nature (park) designers, ecologists and rangers, researchers, activists and spokespersons of the place to global audiences. Although they do not stop being artists, they use their artistic freedom to transgress the other disciplines and bring their approaches to them.

Local in the Global Flow: Critical Tourism, Post-colonial and Post-socialist

If one wishes to look critically at artist-hosting, residencies also serve as a new type of soft colonialism and as artist tourism. Some of the residencies exploit the place and its resources for the sake of the ones in power or with knowledge. This happens quite often in some parts of Asia, South America, Africa, and in Eastern Europe, which is still appealing for artists from the 'former West' because of exoticism and some wilderness, chaotic everydayness and sometimes sincerity and hospitality of a small place. Since postcolonial countries are constantly being decolonized and lots of them are included in global art markets (Global South), the former post-soviet and post-socialist countries from the Balkans to the Baltic countries should also be treated as a legacy of another type of colonialism imposed on them by their neighbours and their ideologies. In theory, these countries and practices were being westernized and connected to the global network probably as 'Global South-East Europe' or 'Global East'[5] over the past three decades. However, these attempts were not always so successful or fast enough and their mentality is still in transition. International residency programmes help to 'normalize' this and include these countries and their specific places with their resources into the international flows of value.

This also influences the practitioners of community art, which has difficulties in being applied in small communities all around the world but especially in 'post-' countries. Due to this exhausting flow of incoming artists some small village communities have already started closing their doors because they do not need another 'passer-by-researcher' who wants to help the secluded community 'to overcome their isolation' and capitalize their knowledge to the artwork later presented in the art market.

Does the local community need artists who arrive to the place as short-time residents? They may be treated as long-term tourists but they are still short-term inhabitants. How many months, years, or decades do you need to spend in a secluded village in the forest, by the sea, or in the dessert to be included in the local community? What is the 'local community' from the power gaze in the post-colonial world? Does it exist or is it another way of framing 'the otherness', capitalize it and include in the global flows of the art market. By 'art market' I mean here not only the commercial representation and sales of artworks but also the production of value in exchange and communication of art and related discourse in public institutions. What do international artists deliver to local community and place? Is it sustainable for hundreds of visiting artists to exploit dozens of local inhabitants? There are many more questions than answers. Each case is very different but has to be really carefully discussed before starting community-oriented or participatory art practices in remote places. Language is also a very important factor of success or failure, especially if a resident is from monolingual countries (mainly Anglo-Saxon). Some of them do not even realize that they cannot work with a local community and come into contact with their native language—they assume 'that everybody speaks English or some other common foreign language'.

In the case of remote residencies, the relationship of the guest and the local, the newcomer and old inhabitant has to be discussed too. Quite a few remote residencies are located in attractive places (nature parks, beaches, mountains) and resort-like settings and their surroundings attract a continuous flow of tourists. Their experiences transform the place with the power of the outsider's gaze.

Some of these issues I have already discussed in my book about critical tourism *Tourists like Us: Contemporary Art and Critical Tourism*, which critically re-approached how the touristic gaze changes the local understanding of the place as well as how local communities and nature are invented and constructed. Quite a few site-specific art projects dealt with these issues, pointed to urgencies and speculated about ways to solve them. For example, a participatory performance during the 4th Inter-format Symposium on Flux of Aquatic and Sand Ecosystems[6] invited participants with brooms to sweep out tourists' footsteps on the sand and help the management of the National Park to restore the wildness of sand dunes.

One of the ways to reduce these obstacles and immerse into local place and community is to facilitate long-term residencies, which start from three or even six months. Certainly, there are quite a few challenges, but they are worth facing and solving. First of all, it is not easy to find artists who will have the time and commitment to stay for such a long time in a remote place; secondly, it is not easy to secure long-term funding. A second option is to support returning residents who over time develop a deep connection with the place or local community and this ensures bilateral exchange. This worked quite well in the Nida Art Colony and returning artists produced substantial and rooted final works during their second and third stays. They participated with their artworks in exhibitions, symposiums, publications and local festivals both in the residency and outside. A third option is collaboration with local artists or practitioners if there are any in such a small and remote place. However, due to the small local community most of the artists always end up with the same collaborators and we are back into an exploitative loop. Indeed, very few artists manage to remove the 'contemporary art' mask from their faces and practices when collaborating with local practitioners and audiences.

Another tendency is that artists, curators, and organizers from old colonialist countries come to countries without a residency culture (like China, Brazil, Russia, and so on) and open up a residency there to host artists from their countries and organize exchanges. I am not saying that they are not of good will and help to make the local context more international as well as organize opportunities for local artists to go abroad, but there is a danger to turn this kind of activity, instead of exchange, into the trade of local exoticism and not-yet-discovered culture and localness. This tendency can also be observed in the new post-WW II economies that never had colonies but today are active players in global cultural export and exchange.

That's how postcolonial and post-socialist countries are involved in the global art market and residencies here serve as hubs to facilitate exchange and import residents in a role of global citizens. Of course, they make the local art scene more international and global, but how many of them overcome the lure of the place and abandon the neo-colonial and touristic gaze? The same question may be asked in return when a residency is organized with exchange back to the 'Western countries'. What are the main motives of hosting these artists besides the fact that the practice of the arriving artists is here better supported and sometimes protected from violation of the freedom of speech in their home country?

These questions could be easily addressed to big and established institutions throughout the world. The bigger or stronger the country, the bigger its art centres, the further corners in the world it reaches and facilitates exchange with. In opposition to them some artist- or community-run residency programmes really find critical importance of international interactions for their organized rooted residency programmers, but they often lack resources and recognition of these exchanges.

Concluding Remarks on Curated Remoteness and Absolute Hospitality

This essay based on practice and specific experiences might also serve as a model for yet-to-come remote residency. But it also refers to lived-through examples of running a residency. Remoteness of the residency is defined both through mental and physical aspects and both support each other. It is very difficult to detach oneself from the hectic tempo of production in one's own studio in the urban metropolis, but as soon as you travel for a considerable amount of time and step out of your new residency studio into an empty village, forest, or beach, you are brought into the mode of deceleration. To support this mode of travel to a remote place and back from to the closest metropolis, which has everything artists need, within one day should be (nearly) impossible.

Remote residency is at once rooted locally and connected globally. Therefore, it is able to provide the balance between the inside and outside, between in-depth and long-lasting relationships. The travel mode to the residency should be also slow because when you travel fast, you miss the details.

The retreat mode in the residency also brings detachment from market and professional competitiveness and is able to provide a safe and comfortable space for artists to experiment and try out new ideas.

Audience is one of the biggest challenges for remote residencies, but first of all do they need an audience? Some of the residency programmes do not for sure. And this is one of their advantages–providing temporary safe space for artist to experiment, to produce, or to retreat. Why desperately try to make community-related art and try to reach audiences, when you can enjoy the solitude and luxurious space of being on your own?

Last but not least, when you are running a residency programme in a remote location, you should always follow absolute hospitality guidelines. It means that anybody working in the residency centre should be able to help with any question at any time because in most cases there is a language or culture barrier to solving any kind of practical or conceptual issue on your own.

Moreover, the uncertainty and stress levels of landing in a new location are quite high, and they are more present in a small place than in a vibrant metropolis. Because of the low density of people and limited local services, residency staff and fellows have to be open and ready for any kind of mental and physical fluctuations and emergencies. Most of the time an initial caring act produces a healthy although temporary community within a residency and these connections tend to become strong and long-lasting.

Hospitality from the staff also includes sharing connections and making residents connected both to the local place and global resources of the residency programme. In the end, the balance of remoteness and connectedness is fine-tuned and this produces a really productive and safe environment.

Absolute caring is an outcome of the slowness of the institution because only giving time and taking that time can produce this situation which otherwise, in a metropolis, would be disrupted by curatorial visits, various meetings, and day and night programmes.

In the end, all the shortcomings of the remoteness in a carefully designed faraway residency programme are turned into advantages both for the artists and for the place itself. The physical presence in a periphery is combined with globally networked hubs and this complex provides slow but exceptional experience and outcomes.

Notes

1 Black Mountain College was an experimental college founded in 1933 by John Andrew Rice, Theodore Dreier, and several others. Based in Black Mountain, North Carolina, the school was ideologically organized around John Dewey's principles of education, which emphasized holistic learning and the study of art as central to a liberal arts education (Source: Wikipedia).

2 Although this concept was popping up from time to time in various conversations about residencies, there was not yet that much reflection on it. Post-rural in this context means that despite being remote and based in a former rural place, you are still connected to relevant global flows. Another aspect here is that there is a tendency of transformation of rural condition in villages and small towns which are being re-populated by people from urban locations. Although some of them still practice agriculture related activities, they are mostly related to ecological and craft economies rather than to what is traditionally understood as leading a villager's life. This trend is especially visible in Nordic-Baltic countries but also in other parts of Europe. Moreover, quite a lot of villages are not inhabited permanently and are now used as summer retreats. Some of the rural places also have very motivated communities of highly educated professionals. These kind of factors enable remote residencies to thrive.

3 Michelkevičius 2013.

4 Extensive discussion can be found in the chapter 'Invented Nature' in Martini and Michelkevičius 2013.

5 'The demise of the Second World's political project–communism–wiped the East off the global map, any distinctiveness of more than 70 years of communist rule erased. The East is too rich to be a proper part of the South, but too poor to be a part of the North. It is too powerful to be periphery, but too weak to be the centre. Power relationships run every which way. The East includes both colonisers and colonies, aggressors and victims; some countries were both at the same time (Tlostanova 2008).' Müller 2018.

6 More about it http://nidacolony.lt/en/projects/symposium/inter-format-symposium-2014.

Literature

— Antanavičiūtė, Rasa, and Vytautas Michelkevičius. 'An Interview/Case Study on Nida Art Colony in the Context of Residencies in Lithuania and Eastern Europe.' In *RE-tooling RESIDENCIES: A Closer Look at the Mobility of Art Professionals*, edited by Anna Ptak, pp. 158–67. Warsaw: CCA Ujazdowski Castle, 2011. www.re-tooling-residencies.org/resources/book.

— Martini, Federica, and Vytautas Michelkevičius, eds. *Tourists Like Us: Critical Tourism and Contemporary Art*. Vilnius: Vilnius Academy of Arts Press/Sierre: ECAV, 2013.

— Michelkevičius, Vytautas. 'Artistic Research in the Green Cube.' In *Tourists Like Us: Critical Tourism and Contemporary Art*. Vilnius: Vilnius Academy of Arts Press/Sierre: ECAV, 2013.

— Müller, Martin. 'In Search of the Global East: Thinking between North and South.' *Geopolitics* 4 April 2018. Available at SSRN: https://ssrn.com/abstract=2881296.

— *Nida Art Colony Log* 3, no. 3 (Autumn 2011–Spring 2012). Also available at http://nidacolony.lt/images/log03.pdf.

Embedding/ Embedded… A Residency Perspective from New York

Livia Alexander &
Nathalie Anglès

In early 2018, the New York City Department of Cultural Affairs announced four new yearlong public artist residencies (PAIR) embedding artists within its various civic agencies to address pressing problems of public policy and governance. Being 'in residence' in New York City, and being embedded 'in residency' at a municipal agency or elsewhere are inextricably linked by the fine threads that enmesh artists in the city's urban fabric. It is indicative of a broader shift that emphasizes the qualities of artistic process as a methodology and an everyday practice; it is one that takes art out of studios, museums and galleries into city agencies, tech companies, public plazas and neighbourhoods. It is what makes twenty-first-century cities great by having the potential of touching the lives of their residents, by infusing artists' soft skills of innovation, problem solving and outside the box thinking into what we do and how we work. But as we know from New York City, desirable cities can also be prohibitively expensive for most artists to live in.

Residency Unlimited (RU) is a modestly sized arts organization based in Brooklyn, New York, that fosters residencies for local and international artists and curators with yearly programs incorporated into its mission. Established in 2009, RU is characterized by a wide footprint that is made possible through the organization's extensive network of collaborations. RU is less focused on the notion of space generally associated with artistic residencies than on providing a tailored approach and the creation of customized environments through a concerted strategy of resource sharing, from collaborating with other art organizations, when an artist needs an individual studio space for example, to mounting exhibitions and other public programmes, and more.

Early on, RU's interest in alternative residency models led to RU Dialogues, an online platform to publish selected and commissioned critical writings on the evolving field of art residencies. The notion of 'embedded' artist residencies and the role of the arts in the future of cities has been one of the long-term areas of interest for RU. A case in point is the symposium 'Embedded, Embedding: Artist Residencies, Urban Placemaking and Social Practice'.[1] Topics put forth at the symposium addressed how collaborative institutional infrastructures between mainly US-based non-profit, governmental, business and creative sectors are being developed through artist residencies as a site of new modelling for support in areas of social practice, creative placemaking and industry collaborations. Speakers came from a wide range of backgrounds, including governmental representatives from the New York City Department of Cultural Affairs who presented PAIR (Public Artists in Residence), which vies to be a model that seeks to embed artists within local civic agencies to nurture and support artistic practice while addressing pressing social and civic issues. PAIR offers artists a fully funded yearlong residency as they work with: the Department of Probation, NYC Commission on Human Rights, the Mayor's Office to Combat Domestic Violence, the Department of Veterans Affairs, the Mayor's Office of Immigrant Affairs. In 2018, the New York City's Department of Correction (DOC) selected the RU artist Onyedika Chuke to conduct research and gain access to detainees, correction officers and policy makers at Rikers Island, New York City's main jail complex. His comments relating to his experience are relevant as we attempt to unravel the complex node of questions raised.

Urban Placemaking

Against the premise of urban placemaking as an aspirational strategy to generate 'vibrancy' in communities through artist residencies, RU submitted four questions to dozens of contributors from all over the world.[2] The answers to date offer insight into one of the main areas of investigation undertaken, namely the present ethical and social role of artist residencies that are being developed in contemporary society (in our case the urban context). These lead questions centred on examining what role can urban planning and cultural policies play in navigating the slippery boundaries between nurturing artistic agency and social engagement, and advancing broader policy initiatives of urban economic growth. Does the artist residency model offer the appropriate conceptual setting for effective implementation? Socially engaged practice further implies work with communities and the necessity for duration and time if meaningful work is to be done. With today's ubiquitous emphasis on measurable outcomes, we asked our contributors what criteria, if any, should be used in assessing embedded artist residencies goals vis-à-vis results? Is there a 'perfect' duration of a residency? When is time 'long enough'? We further sought to explore the monetary and/or social value of artistic labour and how it might be shifting with artists who are increasingly being recognized not only in the aesthetic realm, but also for their capacity to present solutions to everyday questions. Finally, we were interested in asking which embedded artist residency models are currently working effectively? How can we develop more cooperative models that support artistic practice, protect the integrity of the artists, and allow for business development and community innovation?

Whilst the three roundtable responses published to date[3] express varying viewpoints that clearly stem from diverging geographical situations and socioeconomic cultural contexts, they all agree that artist residencies are more and more commonly integrated into urban placemaking as a potent conduit to the development of innovative cultural strategies. In issue #1, Anat Litwin discussed her perspective based on her HomeBase Project, a nomadic artist-run art residency and research programme devoted to a site-specific exploration of the notion of 'home'. She argues that 'while the fear of instrumentalizing art residencies for market needs is relevant, the artist-run residency model is actually not as vulnerable as it seems. It itself can be seen as an instrument towards a much larger creative goal–the creation of an urban life environment is as a total work of art.'[4] Ana López-Ortego of the Bogota-based architecture collective Arquitectura Expandida reflected on the question of time once their ongoing processes of community engagement shifted to a project developed as part of an artistic residency in a Parisian suburb. Because the extension of the residency can often determine the intensity and depth of the process, she indicates the collective's decision to re-direct their focus on developing a tactical strategy rather than designing this or that object.[5] In the upcoming issue on the value of artistic labour, Jianru Wu addresses the impact of the recent large-scale government clean-up of the 'low-end population', resulting in the closure of artist studios and fabrication facilities in Beijing and Shanghai and pushing them to the periphery of the city. As Wu points out, the discourse of extreme class differentiation brought on by the three-to-nine-tiered schema of the 'low-end populations',[6] sparks key questions about the fraught place of art and artists in Chinese society.

While urban placemaking aspires to generate 'vibrancy' in communities through art initiatives and residencies, one persistent key question is who are these programmes really benefiting? What role could or should artists/curators/arts institutions take in shaping policy, be it political, social, economic, or cultural? How much weight do communities these programmes seek to serve have in the process? Funders, bureau-planners, and politicians are drawn to the potential of the arts as a means to create safer communities with better public education, and increased economic growth. In today's climate, such trends not only run the risk of inadvertently, or perhaps not so inadvertently, functioning as a cultural façade for gentrification and community displacement. As scholar Jaime Peck pointed out in his 2005 critique of Richard Florida's controversial book *The Rise of the Creative Class* such an approach comes with political ambiguity that 'mixes cosmopolitan elitism and pop universalism, hedonism and responsibility, cultural radicalism and economic conservatism...' But more importantly, Peck points out the creative trickle-down approach of such initiatives, subordinating the needs of the less privileged to those driving economic development.[7]

In urban environments, the majority of residencies are created and operated by those that have the means to obtain funding, often those that are economically better off. This creates a disadvantage to those desiring to create more grassroots-oriented residencies and programming. In that respect, the residency sphere can be seen as a direct reflection on the current neoliberal late-capitalism broader system. Existing on the same system of hierarchies, it is a sphere that nonetheless assumes a stance that it is operating within a different set of rules. It is therefore imperative that we admit to these similarities and then work towards a more inclusive dialogue. We must forego the age-old model of placing residencies in poor neighbourhoods, e.g. art colonization, for a more inclusive approach of long-term partnership.

How can we harness the new force of invested interest in the arts as a positive force of placemaking without displacing communities and artists out of residence? The answer is rather simple: civic policy that enhances quality of life and creative access to all, a policy that protects the rights and livelihood of all residents. An urban fabric beaming with art and creativity at every cell and corner of its expanse is a win-win for all: policy makers, real estate developers, artists, and residents.

New York City is part of a growing number of American cities–Austin, Boston, Los Angeles among them–deploying such initiatives, while remunerating artists for their work. Reviewing a similar initiative launched by the city of Austin, Texas, in 2015 for the popular online arts magazine *Hyperallergic* critic Claire Voon writes 'Austin's addition to this growing roster exemplifies the value of social practice and the tangible impact artists can have on their communities with their particular skills and ways of thinking.' Tom Finkelpearl, New York City's Commissioner of Cultural Affairs similarly points out that 'art and culture can provide a powerful means for achieving positive social change and improved wellbeing.'

But What About Artists' Wellbeing?

The embedding of artists in these new models of urban art residencies marks a significant move away from the traditional notions of residencies, which focuses on the artist, as opposed to on the community, problem to be resolved, or service to be provided. Mundane, quotidian, durational and slow to unfold, such practices can also stand in sharp contrast to the spectacle and the spectacular that might be sought after by urban planners, or those that we have come to recognize with other art exhibition avenues–the museum, the art fair, or the biennale. They might equally not always align with immediate outcomes sought after by civic agencies and business entrepreneurs looking to team up with artists.

As we worked on this article, we chose to incorporate insightful comments from the New York-based artist and RU Alum Onyedika Chuke. Chuke was one of the four artists selected in 2018 to carry out a yearlong residency within the DOC/Rikers Island. As mentioned, PAIR is a model that seeks to both nurture and support artistic practice while addressing civic issues through creative practice. The process consists of several stages of implementation. First, a research phase, where the appointed artists get to know the agency staff and how they operate while also introducing their artistic practice and process to the staff members. This initial phase is then followed by a proposal outlining one or more public-facing participatory projects to be implemented during the remainder of the residency.

The feedback we are sharing consists of his ongoing experience at New York City's DOC/Rikers Island, how he views the impact of residencies on his artistic career, and more general comments about residency programmes. As an artist who values research as an integral part of his practice, Chuke emphasizes how the DOC residency clearly offers a unique funded opportunity with the support of personnel needed to engage the history, architecture, and infrastructure of the penal system. Chuke finds this aspect of the residency to be significantly vital for his artistic development During the second phase, Chuke intends to collaborate with personnel and inmates on Rikers Island inspired by PAIR's goal to 'offer avenues for self-expression and healing, to create access to art, and to open dialogue between policymakers and those in their custody'.

With the challenges facing artists in urban areas marked by booming real estate markets and a high cost of living, Chuke makes the point that artists need to become better aware of how residencies are created, funded, and managed in order to be truly beneficial to them. The fact is that in the USA, the best residencies are funded by real estate developers and various foundations with motives that do and sometimes do not align with the missions of the residencies. A great part of this is also acknowledging that the term 'artists' is assumed to be general and homogenizing. In reality, gender, race, age, and sexual preference are often determining factors in determining which artists receive opportunities in said residencies.

Chuke also points out how in the creation of urban art residencies, there is also the unfortunately all too prevalent pitfall of economic bias and lack of acknowledgment of pre-existing community-based programmes usually in place before arts groups seek to establish residencies in supposed 'underserved' areas. In many cases, funding or personnel is not given directly to the programmes. Instead, incoming groups employ a more colonial approach that often spurs on gentrification through the displacement of those that are in so-called 'underserved areas'. Often, statements such as 'nothing was here before' are used to describe conditions before artists and residencies arrive in low-income urban areas. The term at once tries to justify the implied elevated status of the artist and then validates impending gentrification of the local. In an ongoing vicious cycle, neighbourhoods are rezoned, the city issues building permits to developers to build new condos and new amenities, the neighbourhood becomes attractive to higher income individuals, prices go up, long-time poorer residents have to leave, and eventually artists themselves are forced out.

In this article we chose to focus more specifically on the topic of embedded artist residencies within the urban fabric as an increasingly popular strategy employed for problem solving/solution finding, and the underlying accompanying motivations, positive and negative. Zooming in on Chuke's personal experience as an artist sheds light onto the residency matrix as a complex web of conflicting socio-economic and cultural conditions in which artists are expected to navigate without necessarily having a clear grasp of the situation in which they find themselves.

Expanding forward and as a possible conclusion, the knowledge that the structures of the art world are flawed can also be liberating to artists and encourage them to take control of their own lives and careers. In a study led by Creative Independent, when 1,016 practicing visual artists from all over the world were asked to reflect on the economics of making art, it comes as no surprise that the majority don't live off their art. More interestingly, when artists were asked to evaluate the structures of the art world, artist residencies turn out to be a much more popular source of support than gallery representation or art school.[8] There is undoubtedly no stronger testimony to the continuously evolving role of residencies as a vital structural pillar of the art ecosystem.[9]

Notes

1 Organized by RU with Livia Alexander (curator, writer, and Chair of the Department of Art and Design at Montclair State University) in February 2017 at The New School/ Parsons MFA Fine Arts Program (New York). For more information about the symposium and a complete list of speakers visit: www.residencyunlimited.org/dialogues/embedded-embedding/.

2 Following the symposium, RU organized in a second phase a series of a yearlong global online roundtables with the support of Artseverywhere. The questions were formulated by Livia Alexander.

3 To access the publication, please visit: www.residencyunlimited.org/dialogue/panels/. The series of roundtables can also be found at www.artseverywhere.ca.

4 http://artseverywhere.ca/2017/11/17/artist-residency-and-the-city/, accessed 23 September 2018.

5 http://artseverywhere.ca/2018/04/17/residency-unlimited-3/, accessed 23 September 2018.

6 The three-to-nine-tiered schema refers to a widely-circulated post dissecting current Chinese class structure into nine tiers, with the three most affluent depicted as the 'ruling class' and the three least affluent as the 'underclass'. The division is based on political power and connections as much as on wealth and prestige. https://foreignpolicy.com/2014/04/25/chinas-new-class-hierarchy-a-guide/.

7 Jaime Peck, 'Struggling with the Creative Class', *International Journal of Urban and Regional Research* 29, no. 4 (December 2005), pp. 740–70, p. 741, 766.

8 Creative Independent, 'Survey Report: A Study on the Financial State of Visual Artists Today', September 23, 2018. https://thecreativeindependent.com/notes/a-study-on-the-financial-state-of-visual-artists-today/.

9 Benjamin Sutton, 'Artists Support Themselves Through Freelance Work and Don't Find Galleries Especially Helpful, New Study Says', *Hyperallergic*, 14 June 2018. https://hyperallergic.com/447056/economics-visual-artist-study-creative-independent/.

Part 5

Transitions

Yours, in Solidarity

Donna Lynas

Over the past ten years, artist residencies have become central to Wysing Arts Centre's work; they drive the public exhibitions and events programmes and affect how the institute operates. The change that artists have made on the institute of Wysing, and what the organization values, by participating in residencies and bringing critical thinking to the organization, cannot be overstated. Artists drive what takes place externally in our public programmes, but they also challenge, and improve, institutional behaviour and thinking.

When artists come to work at Wysing they are here to pursue open-ended research, without defined outcomes, with our support. Up until recently, residencies were held three times a year, over a two-month period, and three to four artists at a time were provided with accommodation, studio, fee and production budget, and a critical context within which to work. Residencies were themed as a mechanism for drawing artists around a common interest. In more idealistic and less politically charged times, themes reflected literary metaphors, such as The Mirror (2012), or mathematical theories that were developed to reveal the 'truth', as in Convention T (2013).

But huge shifts in global politics have had their impact on Wysing both in the concerns of artists, revealed through their work and working methods, and those of us working at Wysing. During the organization's 25th birthday year, in 2014, we made what could be argued the organization's first direct critical or political gesture in response to an issue felt to be urgent and which could be addressed by us; by programming Wysing's annual music festival under the theme The Future with an all-female and non-binary line-up. As the festival's curator, this decision was taken in response to other festivals, including our own in previous years, that had been male-dominated. The action offered a re-balancing of gender within Wysing's music programming, and a statement of intent on how Wysing's next 25 years would evolve.

Since 2014, Wysing has sought to engage with artists who are active outside the art mainstream, whether due to their work falling between disciplines, or because they have chosen to work outside the established art market, or because they have been excluded by institutional structures due to gender, race, or sexuality.

Hosting artists-in-residence over periods of time, and potentially over multiple visits, with no defined artistic outcomes, has enabled Wysing to become a place where ideas about art and society can be discussed in depth. These discussions take place in studios and around the dining table of the farmhouse, but also through Study Days that are open to the public. Study Days are where ideas that are in-discussion privately are tested publicly, and they are crucial in refining thinking and articulating other opinions and viewpoints. Events often include contributions from individuals with specialisms outside the arts, such as journalism, politics, and environmentalism. In all events we are seeking to include the voices who speak from outside the mainstream and who can bring radical thinking to debates, and to the organization.

In recent years this has become equally true of residencies. We have been fortunate to be able to work with some of the most radical, critical, and indeed in my opinion, ethical, artists of today. These artists have become vital to how Wysing has been developed, bringing ideas initially during residencies, expanding these into learning programmes, bringing their extended networks to the institute, curating aspects of our programme. Since 2014, these ideas have centred on gender, race, and sexuality and more widely on marginalization, institutional structures, and the urgency of developing networks of care and support that challenge these structures.

These ideas are interrogated during residencies and related events and all of us working on Wysing's programme attend every event and listen carefully to what is being discussed, constantly asking what our role as an arts organization can be to effect change. One of the things that we have needed to change of course, an ongoing and unfinished exercise, is ourselves; both personally and our institute. This has meant having conversations about gender pronouns and ensuring everyone working at Wysing respects pronoun choices, through to taking on board criticism when we had thought we had got something right only to find we had handled it entirely wrong. In other words, learning how to be better at what we do.

The willingness of Wysing staff and Trustees to allow, and indeed enable, the artists we work with to have influence over the future direction of the organization is one way to ensure that Wysing is responding to what artists need. In addition, artists have been playing an increasing role in the delivery of programmes. Wysing has nine full-time staff running programmes at the 11-acre Bourn site, alongside a number of ambitious national and international partnerships. In 2017, 98 artists helped us to deliver these programmes through leading our alternative Masters programme, working with us on events and symposia, leading workshops and mentoring programmes.

Operating in this way places Wysing staff very close to art practice and production, which began to raise questions as to whether our fixed residency model was becoming less relevant. Artists were struggling to commit to being in residence for six to eight weeks, and more often than not, were leaving the site to continue teaching jobs and to travel for other projects, or to see their families. We were noticing that artists were spending much of their budgets on travel and time away from Wysing, which affected the dynamic and rhythm of the residencies. This, combined with a growing awareness that there were artists who were not in a position to take up residencies due to disabilities or caring responsibilities confirmed that the residency model we had operated for six years was no longer working.

Alongside this, over the past two years we have tried to find ways to ensure residency opportunities were reaching artists who had either not been supported previously or were those who were operating within wider networks rather than pursuing solo practices. At the end of 2016, we announced the annual theme of Wysing Polyphonic, or 'many voices', and put out a call for applications for residencies for 2017 stating that we wanted to work with a range of artists to explore a diversity of contexts and positions to help better understand the role of art, artists, and arts organizations such as Wysing, at a moment of global political change. We said we would provide both a platform for many voices, in particular those that have the potential to be over-looked in the current political rhetoric, alongside a range of ways that those voices can be heard. Building on a number of events during 2016 that explored alternative sites for community and activism, we sought to build foundations to enable us to work with artists whose work, or whose networks, empowered and supported diverse communities of interest.

This call-out revealed new networks of artists to us and it also enabled other programmes, including the annual music festival which was guest-curated by an artist for only the second time, to also bring artists within their networks that had not had contact with Wysing previously. Our 2017 programme enabled a more nuanced conversation across the year about legibility and how, in engaging many voices, those voices have the right to be heard in the way that they wished. Édouard Glissant's text *Philosophie de la Relation* (Philosophy of the Relation, 2009), which advocates the right to opacity, was a point of reference to many artists across that year.

At the end of 2017 these practical, theoretical and organizational considerations led to a complete re-think of our residency programme. If we had been trying to give more agency to artists in how our institution was operating, how could our residency programme respond to that?

We began by thinking about the residencies in relation to other programmes, including retreats and artist-led masterclasses, which were much shorter in duration and for which we invited an artist to develop a four- to five-day session for ten artists. Introduced in 2009, we had initially curated these retreats ourselves, both in terms of a theme, contributors, and participants but as with other programmes these were increasingly being curated in collaboration with artists. The starting point for the 2018 residency call-out was that we wanted to enable residencies that might last a weekend, a month, two months, a year, or over multiple visits; however long artists think they needed. We didn't have a fixed number of residencies in mind and planned to shape our programme in response to the open call.

In the call-out for 2018 residencies, which was announced in December 2017, we didn't announce a theme, or residency dates as in previous years. Instead we listed what we had to offer artists: a five-bedroomed farmhouse with shared kitchen and bathrooms, that sleeps up to ten people; a self-contained live/work studio that sleeps up to four; three studios; a music/recording studio; a ceramics studio; a large seminar/meeting room; use of a vehicle; funding for fees, production, and travel; access to curatorial and technical staff; an engaged and interested context, including visitors to the site and an online audience.

We also stated that we were interested in hearing from artists who are already working within self-organized groups who would like to use the opportunity to strengthen the group, those who wanted to come together for the first time to collaborate on new ideas, and artists who might want to bring their children or families. And, as with all our programmes, we said we were keen to hear from artists who could bring a range of cultural, social, racial, and gender perspectives to the programme. And that by 'artists' we meant visual artists, musicians, dancers, choreographers, and writers, or those working in other disciplines that have a strong connection to the visual arts.

From this open call forty artists were selected to be in residence across the year. This included a number of new artist-networks who wanted the opportunity to return to the site three or four times across the year, enabling them to re-group and develop and strengthen the network. These networks included a group of artists living and working with, often hidden, disabilities; artists who were exploring the legacies of cyberfeminism; and those who had formed a new network for artists of colour. We also hosted artists who were able to bring their families, again over shorter multiple periods, instead of one long fixed residency duration. Offering artists the opportunity to choose who to be in-residence with has also made the residency more efficient, with less time spent on getting to know one another, and to work out domestic and cleaning arrangements. It has also offered the institution the opportunity to have repeat engagement with artists and enabled us to have ongoing and longer-term conversations with them, both in how their work and network have developed, and in how Wysing could continue to find ways to support them into future years.

Although we didn't announce a theme for the 2018 residencies, there was one: Yours, in solidarity. It was never stated as a theme but the manner in which the call-out had been worded, implied that we wanted to give over our resources, in solidarity, to artists who wanted to make change, for themselves and their extended networks. Perhaps due to the previous year's interrogation of opacity it felt wrong to overstate the intention, but rather to act on it.

'Yours, in solidarity' is a statement of intent. *Yours in Solidarity* is also a film and an ongoing work by artist Nicoline van Harskamp which was screened at Wysing in 2014.

About Wysing Arts Centre

Wysing Arts Centre is a thriving cultural campus of ten buildings across an 11acre rural site hosting experimental residencies for UK and international artists and delivering a critically acclaimed public programme of gallery exhibitions and events, including conferences, symposia, workshops and music events. Through consistently innovative programming, Wysing influences the development of the visual arts in the UK, Europe and, increasingly, the wider world. Operating outside the usual gallery system and urban context, Wysing's unique position enables it to develop programmes that provide opportunities for the exchange of knowledge and ideas and which interrogate the role of art, artists, and arts organizations in contemporary society; acting as a testing ground for ideas that are fed productively back into the mainstream through the organization's extensive networks and partnerships.

Divided We Move Together

Artists at Risk (AR) at the Interface of Human Rights and the Arts

Ivor Stodolsky &
Marita Muukkonen
(in alternating order)

In our neo-nationalist times, non-Western art practitioners are far from privileged 'global citizens' who can travel the world at will. Art professionals and intellectuals, from crises regions in particular, face formidable barriers erected by governments in the form of national migration offices and their visa policies. Especially the West maintains a 'hostile environment'[1] in the infamous phrase of Theresa May's regime, for those arriving from 'difficult' regions of the world. 'Divided we move', as the sociologist Zygmunt Bauman succinctly put it long ago.[2]

After a brief introduction on mobility in the arts, this essay will discuss the cases of artists from these 'difficult' regions. For it is precisely those—such as Syria, Kurdish Turkey, Egypt, Yemen or Zimbabwe—which our organization Artists at Risk (AR) maintains a keen focus on.

Mobility: A Preamble

Since at least the eighties, so-called nomadism and mobility have been key concepts in the discourse of contemporary art. The post-structuralist theoretical agenda intentionally blurred the notions of centre and periphery, and indeed, as compensation for its earlier neglect, the periphery became valorized as more interesting or important. The language of freedom and flows, the democratization of movement, speed and flexibility, swarms and rhizomes were on everyone's lips, from fashionable philosophers to their countless epigones and artistic followers.

With time, however, moving out of an earlier romantic 'underground' or 'subversive' scene, the 'nomad' became the fashionable picture of the artist as constantly on the move, hopping from project to project, artist-in-residency to artist-in-residency, from biennial to biennial. As more and more artists were invited to a burgeoning number of artist-in-residencies—seeking new experiences, inspiration or to realize site-specific work—they became part of a global jet set, more recently democratized by low-budget airlines. This was the experience of being on the move, of travelling light, of readiness for change and new encounters.

With the general expansion of this model, however, the initial goal of openness and re-evaluation of perspectives was encroached upon by a more purely entrepreneurial ethos. Neoliberal economic pressures re-moulded mobility in its own image, generating a form of 'mobility for paid mobility's sake'. What Eve Chiapello and Luc Boltanski termed 'the project regime'—in which mobility, creativity, speed and flexibility are sold at a premium, and community is at best only temporary–was a clear expression of what they described as 'the new spirit of capitalism'.[3] In short, the initial joy, or even transgressive *jouissance* (to employ the once fashionable Lacanian term) of 'crossing borders', has been appropriated as hackneyed marketing term and business concept in the neoliberal language of 'creative industries'.

Here the ecology of mobility must be mentioned, even if in passing. Climate change is undoubtedly the cardinal question of our time, and yet there are only extremely rare cases of artists who simply do not fly. For unfortunately this choice, too, is a luxury for the majority constrained by the project regime: copious time and often much higher costs are the price of alternative forms of travel.

A further wholly different vantage point is given by the post-colonial predicament. Artists from formerly colonized countries have historical and living relations to diasporas situated around the world and vice versa. For them, mobility can be a socio-cultural necessity. Conversely, for peoples of European descent, there is an injunction to re-think the world beyond the Eurocentric paradigm, and hence geography.

In short, mobility today is often not simply a matter of choice. It is predicated upon the need to 'be where it happens'–that is, at key events in the art world and/or deep within networks in the national/diaspora context. Personal relationships with colleagues, institutions, and funders are crucial and almost impossible to access without travelling to and from peripheries to centres. And of course, the ongoing explosion of biennials, festivals, fairs and residencies–the *de facto* workplace for international art practitioners–continues to raise the *requirement* for mobility.

Artists at Risk

In great parts of the world, artists, writers, curators, and critics are targets of politically motivated threats and persecution. From its inception, our curatorial collective Perpetuum Mobile (PM) has been working in regions with histories of authoritarian repression. We have worked with individuals, collectives, and movements whose artistic expression has been threatened, violated, or censored, or whose work may otherwise have been lost to (art) history. PM's larger thematic streams have included 1) a focus on the late-Soviet underground and Putin-era dissident art, 2) a focus on artists of Romani origin, 3) research on the revolutions and uprisings in the Arab world and globally, post-2011, from the Indignados, to Occupy, to Gezi Park and 4) our more recent work with non-conformist and oppositional artists at risk worldwide. Quite naturally, a concern for safety grew out of these multiple-iteration curatorial processes. Developing over several years, our work resulted in Artists at Risk (AR), a network institution comprised of residency programmes across Europe and strategies for heightened mobility: a fast-reaction platform for art practitioners under threat.

The primary motivation for mobility and temporary relocation of AR Residents is to enable them take a 'breather' in a safe place. An AR Residency is a usually 3–12 month 'stepping stone' towards a continued *professional* artistic and engaged practice. AR Residents explicitly do *not* come to Europe to seek asylum or refugee status. They usually have a clear intention of returning to their countries of origin, and in fact, due to their active engagement and courage in confronting social and political issues, AR Residents often figure as points of reference in their societies of origin. Often, they represent what we have called 're-aligned'[4] agencies of change–rejecting multiple hegemonic means of societal control such as religious fundamentalism, leadership cults or elite-serving economic ideologies, while advocating paths for a common good. Despite being censored, silenced, or tortured, AR Residents may return to play a significant part of rebuilding their often conflicted or war-torn societies.

Obtaining visas to enter 'fortress Europe' is one of Artists at Risk 's biggest challenges. In the current climate of institutionalized xenophobia, European governments are closing doors not only to desperate refugees, but also to renowned cultural figures going through the proper consular offices and procedures.[5, 6] So, despite the 'round-trip' mobility of AR candidates, visa processes are often gruelling, and the outcomes are not always positive. For these reasons, AR is currently developing residencies in non-Schengen European areas and on other continents, although funding and hosting, especially for dissident art practitioners, is a challenge.

Heavy Travelling

The difficulty of travel can be prohibitive for AR candidates, and visa policies and procedures too often seem created for no better reason than to create heavy logistic and financial obstacles. Finnish visas for Syrians are not issued by the Embassy in the neighbouring city of Beirut, for example, but only in Ankara, the distant capital of Turkey—excluding from Finland all Erdogan-critics with a Turkish travel ban, aside from all those without sufficient funds.

It took a whole year to procure a three-month Finnish Schengen visa for Issa Touma, an internationally renowned Syrian photographer and short-film maker. He finally became an AR-Safe Haven Helsinki resident in 2014. This allowed him to digitalize his photo-archive and initiate work on his film *9 Days: From My Window in Aleppo*, which in 2017 won the BFI London Film Festival Award as well as the European Short Film Prize. AR helped Touma find a two-year residency in Sweden, and throughout this time, despite the war, he travelled back and forth to Aleppo, to organize his Art Camping festival, a series of art activities for youth, and especially young women in Aleppo.

It is an important part of the mandate of AR to work with art-practitioners as art professionals before, during, and after their AR Residencies. Their artistic practice is usually not supported by their countries, but can often benefit them greatly. Since spring 2018, Issa Touma returned to Syria permanently, re-launching his International Photo Festival in Aleppo. He is particularly critical of organizations that encourage a one-way 'brain drain'. Artists and intellectuals, he argues, have a role in conflict regions to rebuild the ethical, civil, and artistic fabric of life.

Fascism Then and Now

During the nightmare of state fascism of the thirties, many artists and intellectuals such as Walter Benjamin, Marc Chagall, Max Ernst, André Breton, and Hannah Arendt sought to escape Nazi Europe. Many more of them would have met an early death without the work of underground activists such as Hans and Lisa Fittko[7] and their colleague Varian Fry of the Emergency Rescue Committee.[8] Only a few years earlier, during the Spanish Civil War, the poet Pablo Neruda organized a ship from fascist Spain to Chile saving anti-Franco intellectuals. Legendary new art movements and institutions such as Black Mountain College (with many émigré students and faculty from Bauhaus),[9] the New School in New York (Arendt, Adorno) or the Institute for Advanced Study in Princeton (Einstein, Gödel) were created by the intellectual and artistic force of these immigrants. Today's philosophy, science, and art are unimaginable without them.

Extreme repressive ideologies and fascism are on the rise again today. If we are to avoid a century as catastrophic as the last, intellectuals and art practitioners must feel empowered to take risks, speak up, and confront the rise of violent intolerance, censorship, and war. Access to international mobility, assistance, and support affords courage to those upholding artistic and intellectual currents vital to non-repressive political cultures. Artists at Risk (AR) is conceived as a global network of interlinked residencies, enabling fast-reaction responses, on the background of this darkening political horizon.

Network-Institutions and the 'Helsinki Model'

Artists at Risk grew out of the need to provide 'breathers' for visual art practitioners at risk with whom we were working as curators. It was a bottom-up necessity of our curatorial platform Perpetuum Mobile (PM), which founded and runs residencies for artists at risk since 2013. The residents were invited through PM's peer-networks, the result of years of curatorial and residency practice, and hosted and funded in partnership with the Helsinki International Artist Programme (HIAP). The street artist Ganzeer and the 'Singer of Tahrir Square' Ramy Essam, both leading artists of the Egyptian revolution of 2011, were among the first residents at our first 'Safe Haven' on the island of Suomenlinna (in the former premises of NIFCA) in Helsinki. In cooperation with national and municipal politicians and dozens of artists, activists, and civil society institutions, PM succeeded in establishing a sustainable, long-term institutional form, financed primarily by the City of Helsinki: Ar-Safe Haven Helsinki.

With this first safe anchoring in Finland, Perpetuum Mobile has been developing and expanding Artists at Risk as an international 'network-institution'. What we call the 'Helsinki Model' provides an example for how to build new residencies-hubs, otherwise known as 'AR Safe Havens', in other localities. A local group of organizers, funders, co-hosts, and artistic and civil society institutions come together to provide a dense web of support, local knowledge, and opportunities.[10] This way, in preparatory and ongoing meetings, we can make sure AR-Residents are welcomed in a social context that enables a crucial web of professional connections and access to local information, venues, job opportunities, and resources.

To the best of our knowledge, AR was the first organization of its kind, locating its activity at the intersection of human rights and the visual arts. It also developed a new residency model and curatorial focus. Filling a gap for those creative intellectuals that fall beyond the remit of organizations such as PEN (writers and journalists), FreeMUSE (monitoring and campaigns) or SafeMUSE (Norwegian residencies for musicians) it is developing a network institution facilitating fast-reaction residencies for art practitioners at risk. Currently, small and larger-scale initiatives are operational or in development in Berlin, Athens, Cambridge UK, western Finland, the Provence, Oslo, Reykjavik, Barcelona, Nigeria and Serbia. We are glad to see lively interest from around the world.

Dissent in the Twenty-first Century

Looking back at the early twenty-first century, the question of 'art and responsibility' pervaded philosophy and artistic practice in both direct (existentialism) and more subtle ways (Dada, Surrealism, and so on). During the Cold War, literature became the art form *par excellence* of dissidence. One need only think of Pablo Neruda, Alexander Solzhenitsyn, or Joseph Brodsky. Can one compare this to Pussy Riot, Ai Weiwei, or even Banksy in our time? It may be too early to tell, but contemporary art may be a template for a dissident genre of the twenty-first century. However evaluated or denigrated, oppressive regimes and their enemies have a way of amplifying oppositional forms of artistic expression.

In fighting oppression, the first to put themselves in harm's way are no doubt dedicated activists, investigative journalists, and their supporters. Artistic dissent can however often bring complex issues to a far broader audience. Creative institutional networks can make sure these dissenting forces can fulfil their vital role. Divided perhaps, but together.

This article was originally commissioned for the publication Residencies Exchange, *Madrid: hablarenarte (forthcoming).*

Notes

1 Martha Bozic, Caelainn Barr, and Niamh McIntyre. Additional reporting by Poppy Noor, 'Revealed: Immigration Rules in UK More than Double in Length', *The Guardian*, 27 August 2018, sec. UK news, www.theguardian.com/uk-news/2018/aug/27/revealed-immigration-rules-have-more-than-doubled-in-length-since-2010.

2 Bauman was referring primarily to class, but race compounds class divisions, as does gender. Zygmunt Bauman, *Globalization: The Human Consequences* (Hoboken: Wiley, 2013), Chapter 4.

3 Luc Boltanski and Ève Chiapello, *The New Spirit of Capitalism* (London: Verso, 2005).

4 'Concept', *The Re-Aligned Project. www.re-aligned.net/concept/, accessed 5 October 2018.*

5 Sian Cain, 'UK Refuses Visas for a Dozen Edinburgh Book Festival Authors', *The Guardian*, 8 August 2018, www.theguardian.com/books/2018/aug/08/visas-refused-for-a-dozen-authors-invited-to-book-festival.

6 See, for example Ari Akkermans, 'The Challenges of Being a Syrian Artist Today', *Hyperallergic*, 19 July 2018, https://hyperallergic.com/452057/the-challenges-of-being-a-syrian-artist-today/.

7 Lisa Fittko, *Escape through the Pyrenees* (Evanston, IL: Northwestern University Press, 2000).

8 Varian Fry, *Surrender on Demand* (New York: Argo-Navis, 2013).

9 Emily J. Levine, 'From Bauhaus to Black Mountain: German Émigrés and the Birth of American Modernism', *Los Angeles Review of Books*, 16 May 2016. https://lareviewofbooks.org/article/bauhaus-black-mountain-germanemigres-birth-american-modernism/, accessed 29 August 2018.

10 Among many others these include the Finnish Artist's Union, Finnish Musicians' Union, Kone Foundation, our co-hosting organizations HIAP-Helsinki International Artist Programme and Villa Eläintarha, the Saari Residence/Saastamoinen Foundation partner residency, PEN-Finland, the Finnish Anna Lindh Foundation, the Finnish Human Rights League as well as pro-bono lawyers and doctors.

Going Post-fossil in a Neoliberal Climate

Jenni Nurmenniemi

What does it mean to go post-fossil? This newly coined concept signifies the shift from burning fossil fuels[1] to using renewable, less polluting options. Importantly, the term also refers to the cultural reconstruction and mental changes that are happening as human societies face the threats of climate breakdown[2] and collapsing ecosystems. The key here is to recognize how the use of fossil fuels has shaped people's experience of the world, of each other, and of themselves—early twenty-first-century societies are largely dependent on it, art not being an exception.

Despite their unevenly distributed effects, the extraction and consumption of fossil fuels have shaped societies everywhere: communication, housing, transportation, and the global economy would all look very different without them. Going post-fossil refers to the attempts to decrease the level of fossil fuel dependency. The continued consumption has devastating effects on the climate and that has ramifications for all aspects of life. The term post-fossil indicates a desire to move beyond the dead end of fossil modernity. This calls for unlearning and rebooting, for a fundamental paradigm shift.

The global influence of neoliberal ideas and policies since the late 1980s is deeply connected with the escalation of climate change. Neoliberalism advocates an unregulated economy, privatization and loosening of state control at all sectors, rapid economic growth and fast profiteering instead of focusing on long-term goals. Thus, it effectively works against all things necessary for the post-fossil transition: more strict regulation and new legislation, binding intergovernmental agreements, supporting climate-friendly practices, and committing to long-term planning.

Over the past three decades, neoliberalism has also had a massive effect on public management and the cultural sector. Even in the Nordic countries, where some public funding for culture still exists despite severe austerity measures, new forms of public management that focus on productivity, efficiency, measurable outcomes and impact, commercial potential and a great turnout, have shifted the way art organizations see themselves and how they operate. This has created a situation in which cultural organizations may find it challenging to commit to long-term planning and projects that do not fit within these parameters.

The post-fossil transition starts by noticing how human existence is completely dependent on the biophysical constraints of our planet. This recognition is only the beginning, and already a major challenge within the field of art—possibly partly thanks to the internalization of the neoliberal ideals, which then fuse together with the persistent claims of art's autonomy from the rest of the world. While on many other fields climate action and post-fossil discourse have already become mainstream, most art organizations seem to be only capable of addressing ecology as a theme. Taking the post-fossil plight seriously means turning away from all the things formerly considered as the criteria for a successful art institution: global networks, presence, and influence. In other words, there is high risk involved. Is acknowledging art's entanglement in worldly processes considered as a threat to creative freedom, or is adopting more sustainable ways of organizing perhaps simply inconvenient?

Major shifts will be happening eventually as the harmful effects of burning the remaining oil, coal, and natural gas unfurl in full intensity. The question is then, what could be done to foster transitions towards livable futures instead of actively contributing to the climate breakdown? However, there is a rather urgent concern that needs to be voiced before continuing. Whenever publicly discussing these projects and subjects, an argument or a question arises from the audience: aren't these concerns only reserved for the privileged? It is true that committing fully to the post-fossil transition is not possible if one is already struggling to make ends meet on a daily basis.

Also, not all voices seem to be taken equally seriously. The theoretical writing on the subject, especially on the need to rethink energy, seems to be dominated by (assumedly) male thinkers of Western origin. If post-fossil is considered, like ecology, as a tool or an operation system instead of as a topic or theme,[3] it starts to reveal its intersectional potential. While it can help in dissecting the underlying assumptions, fallacies, and colonialist modus operandi of fossil modernity, it can turn into a perspective that cuts through a jumble of power relations.

Critical questions related to gender, race, and capitalism are an integral part of the post-fossil transition. It is absolutely necessary to ask who envisions futures and who are being left out? For myself, a post-fossil organization is necessarily also a non-binary feminist one, and codes of conduct for a feminist art organization[4] might also inform the reshaping of the post-fossil organizational framework. Fossil modernity has been built on binary opposites and mechanisms of othering, and there cannot be anything fundamentally different, if this logic is not recognized and replaced.

The Role of Residencies in the Post-fossil Transition

Residencies can play an important part in the post-fossil transition of the cultural field as incubators for new practices and by being an example for other cultural institutions. They may expand the limits of collective imagination within and beyond the art field by showing that it is possible and meaningful to operate in a way that takes the biophysical limits of our planet into consideration.

During residencies, artists and curators often experiment with new ideas and ways of working. By having to adjust to a new environment, they usually need to develop new routines, which they sometimes continue after the residency. Especially in larger residency organizations, where several people work and live in close proximity, the element of peer support (and pressure) may amplify this effect. In this kind of residency context, where people's daily lives and the art community are inseparably connected, it is possible to tackle ecological sustainability and post-fossil transition not just as themes in art. Instead, they can be addressed as aspects of a fundamental paradigm shift—one with potential to change how people see the world and themselves, live their lives, and how art is made and experienced.

The artists, curators, researchers, and writers who take the post-fossil practices along with them from their time in residency, spread these modes of working to other contexts as well. At present, their ideals and principles are mostly not compatible with the majority of art institutions. This can unfortunately come at the cost of being excluded, or may create friction. Adopting new ways of organizing takes extra time and effort, and in the short term it might also seem to cause additional costs to organizations. However, in the long run going post-fossil is probably also the most financially sustainable option.

As an example, my own curatorial practice has developed at HIAP (Helsinki International Artist Programme) through being constantly challenged by artists- and curators-in-residence who have a deep commitment to ecologically viable and meaningful ways of working. The shift in my thinking, and especially in doing, has been a slow and gradual process. The initial spark was a five-year project that focused on the intersections of ecology and art in particular ecosystems across Europe.[5] As an increasing number of cultural workers become openly critical to ecologically unsustainable ways of working, the institutions eventually will have to revise and readjust their codes of conduct.

Residency communities can actively support more symbiotic, symbiogenetic, and 'sympoietic' understandings of the world,[6] where emphasis is placed on collaboration rather than on competition, on co-dependencies instead of relishing in fantasies of independence and self-sufficiency. The above might apply especially to larger residency communities where several people live and work in close proximity, and in which the whole organization is committed to developing post-fossil practices. Under these kinds of conditions the necessary peer support and positive pressure may emerge. But smaller organizations can play an equally important role, given that they either select residents who can push the organization forward, or by deliberately building a residency programme that challenges the residents to revise and adjust their practice.

Why residencies might become potential game changers in the post-fossil shift is because they tend to operate as somewhat undefined structures where art and the everyday, public, and private realms permeate each other. A lot of people come to a residency willing to absorb and cultivate new aspects into their practices.

For residencies both large and small, building networks with like-minded organizations is a great way of building momentum and sharing knowledge and skills. It is equally important to reach out to those bodies that do not share the same concerns, to educate and invite funders and policy-makers to participate in the discussions. There are no guarantees that the call will be answered but by sharing, one already implies that a pressing concern exists and is calling for wider attention.

Transitioning: Practical Aspects and Experiments

The post-fossil transition and reconstruction have to be addressed as multi-faceted issues. However, to focus our thoughts and efforts while trying to make our residency centre less dependent on the use of fossil fuels, we chose to concentrate on a few key aspects. By changing the ways that our organization deals with energy, transportation, and food, we aim to transform HIAP gradually into a post-fossil residency centre. Travel, especially flying, is the single most fossil fuel-intensive area in the field of residencies and contemporary art more broadly. The ability to move fast from one place to another has defined success in the scene for a long time, and was also imperative to becoming widely recognized. And yet, a single long-distance flight can produce so much CO_2 that it easily nullifies the benefits of all one's climate action. Airline travel immediately multiplies the ecological footprint of individuals and organizations, and even though offsetting emissions is possible, it is a far from perfect solution. Until petroleum-based airplane fuel can be replaced with a renewable option, the only sensible solution is not to fly at all, or choosing very carefully when to fly, staying longer at the destination, compensating the emissions, and traveling light.

Many artists already refuse to fly to a residency or to an exhibition, or to realize a project if its ecological aspects are not properly considered. During the past five years that I have spent working closely with the ecological paradigm shift, encountering these refusals have become increasingly common. For art organizations that operate under the neoliberal paradigm, which emphasizes cost-efficiency from the short-term point of view, this is inconvenient. Organizing complicated travel itineraries involving multi-phased logistics by land and sea demands knowledge, effort, and time. Currently, it is also often more expensive compared to flying.

This should be taken into consideration already while planning projects by applying and allocating more funding for travel, and by considering also the planning phase and actual travel as integral parts of the residency. The residency can already require in their open call or invitation that resident fellows should use alternative means of transportation for flying. For overseas visitors, residencies should be longer and organized in one stretch instead of flying back and forth. For these kinds of longer residencies, Mustarinda and HIAP are also discussing the opportunity to spend time in both residencies as part of one trip. Instead of coercing, the residencies should come up with incentives and support, and additionally develop their own ways of compensating the unavoidable costs to the environment. These guidelines should apply to the staff as well, even though people cannot be expected to travel long distances and to devote weeks to work trips.

Another post-fossil experiment in progress at HIAP aims at increasing the energy awareness within the residency community. This happens through a study conducted in collaboration with Mustarinda, in which the residents can easily follow and affect their own energy consumption at the residency by adjusting thermostats that control the room temperature at their studio and living quarters. This is a pilot study that we hope will give valuable information about people's responses to the possibility to better understand and control their energy consumption. Still, the level of comfort remains in the hands of each resident, so it does not affect their daily life unless they choose so.

There have also been micro experiments and practices related to food. As an example, we have shifted from vegetarian to fully plant-based menus at almost all HIAP community and public events. Attention has been paid to waste management and recycling, and the summer of 2018 also saw a small gardening experiment, with the underlying idea of getting exercise in community gardening and adding a little local fresh produce to our plates. The focus on local produce has to do with trying to become more connected to the residency environment and its traits and dynamics, as well as supporting the local economy, by buying food produced and manufactured in the region whenever possible.

Some energy during the first year of HIAP and Mustarinda's post-fossil transition project has gone into getting to know each other and community-building through shared discussions and reading circles. The two organizations are quite different: Mustarinda is a collective consisting of a large number of volunteers, who take turns in running the Mustarinda House. Their whole operation has been constructed upon the idea of testing practices for the post-fossil transition, whereas HIAP is an association with a changing group of 10–12 people working at two locations, with 70–100 residents annually, in recent years. Ecology or post-fossil transition are not guiding principles at HIAP, instead they have gradually become an important part of the programme.

Since the aim is to turn theory into practice, this project has to be one that everyone in the organization can be part of. Its scope reaches from strategy to programming to the most 'mundane' decisions, or better yet it merges these seamlessly. The organization's rhythms and cycles, the choosing of coffee, dishwashing tablets, biodegradable cups, the selection process and means of travel for the resident artists, thermostats in the studios, ways of communicating the bigger and smaller steps to different stakeholders, all need to be considered. These decisions require discussion and a slowly growing collective knowledge about the consequences of different choices. This is difficult in a situation where only few people work in the organization on a longer-term or fulltime basis, and even with them the work is mostly chopped into separate projects. This creates a challenge to the sharing of practices.

There are also no tools for evaluating a residency centre's ecological impact that would be universally applicable as such. How to measure the change, and also question the quantified, statistical approach as the only indicator of change? All the contexts and factors shaping them are so different that tools such as carbon foot print calculators need to be tailored specifically to each organization.

The Challenge in Being All over the Place

HIAP seems to be currently at the crossroads. While the volume of one of Northern Europe's largest residency programmes has gradually been limited in order to foster more meaningful residency experiences with a more developed sense of community, at the same time the number and scale of international collaboration projects have increased. The collaborative projects, that often take place outside of Finland, have provided opportunities for broadening HIAP's publics and impact. At the same time they have kept our carbon footprint growing, as well as fuelled experiences of being dislocated and dispersed. And even if we would refrain from long-haul travel completely, this feeling of being dispersed is increasingly difficult to avoid:

> Climate change creates a new language, in which you have to be all over the place; you are always all over the place. It makes every animal body implicated in the whole world. Even the patient who is anaesthetised on an operating table, barely breathing, is illuminated by surgeon's lamps which are powered with electricity trailed from a plant which is pumping out of its chimneys a white smoke that spreads itself out against the sky. This is every living thing on earth.[7]

These lines of thought by essayist Daisy Hildyard in *The Second Body* refer to one of the paradoxes of life in the early twenty-first century: while many borders are closing and divisions deepen, things and beings are increasingly connected through the production, distribution, and consumption chains of the global market economy—and its unwanted side effects. Hildyard writes how everyone seems to have a second body, in addition to the first physical one, entangled in globally distributed processes.

Neoliberal and traditional art world fantasies do not seem so different—both often create experiences of dispersion by detaching processes from any particular place, and rendering everything into fragmented forms. This has all kinds of alienating implications for the lived experience. In this situation, Finnish post-fossil philosophers Antti Salminen and Tere Vadén are calling for focality. The concept, borrowed from philosopher Albert Borgmann, refers to the skills and knowledge passed along generations that support sustained, thriving ecosystems in a certain area.[8] This idea could not be more distant from the custom typical of economies of contemporary art that mostly thrive on rapidly changing sceneries. Residency centres, when working in a focused way, in the long term instead of the short cycle, and re-aligned with the principles of focality, may provide testing grounds for challenging this dispersion. However, the neoliberal cultural climate sets up a real challenge to these efforts, as it is in stark contradiction with the post-fossil principles of understanding the multi-layeredness of one's context, of becoming less productive (on the old, fossil-fuelled terms) and thus less harmful to the biosphere.

The climate and ecosystemic breakdown and their ramifications may either unify or divide people, but to address them in any meaningful way requires accepting complexity as the guiding principle. As there are no instant, simple solutions, simplistic articulations will not do. As traditional distinctions and taxonomies become unusable in the wake of climate breakdown, it is necessary to start thinking about the world through, *sympoiesis*, along Donna Haraway's lines of thought, and to reshape ethics and political systems accordingly.[9] The shift to post-fossil culture and societies cannot happen without re-evaluating fundamental concepts such as nature, energy, ecology, and humanity. It is necessary to understand what kinds of ideologies and historical processes have shaped these concepts, and what kinds of power dynamics they reproduce and generate. While striving toward a more liveable planet (and more meaningful lives), the transformation of language, decision-making systems, daily habits and art practices has to be a joint process.

As all big life changes, it is not something that will happen overnight. Instead, as with all major transformations, it is a process that demands exercise in order to become a practice.[10]

Notes

1 Oil, coal, and natural gas.
2 Following artist Brett Bloom's (one of the participants in the project Frontiers in Retreat, 2013-2018) reasoning, I use the term climate 'breakdown' instead of the more generally used climate 'change'. This is because breakdown seems to be a more truthful term in the light of current research on the subject. See more in: Bloom 2015.
3 Media theorist Jussi Parikka writes about ecology as less an analytical concept denoting a thing than a way of looking at things and their relations, seeing it more as an operation. Parikka 2018, p. 85.
4 See, for instance: 'Feminist (Art) Institution: Code of Practice', http://feministinstitution.cz/code-of-practice/ (20 August, 2018).
5 Frontiers in Retreat was a five-year multidisciplinary project coordinated by HIAP–Helsinki International Artist Programme. Its concept was based on the work of curator Taru Elfving and it was curated by Jenni Nurmenniemi alongside the partners from seven residency organizations across Europe. Frontiersinretreat.org (18 September, 2018).
6 Haraway 2017.
7 Hildyard 2017, pp. 13-14.
8 Salminen and Vadén 2015, pp. 76-125.
9 Haraway 2016.
10 Warmest thanks to curator Aleksandra Kiskonen, who coordinated the first steps of the post-fossil transition project at HIAP, in Spring-Summer 2018. Our discussions and her articulations have inspired and informed parts of this text. Her reflections on the project can be found on HIAP Blog: *Where are we now with HIAP's post-fossil transition?* http://hiaphelsinki.tumblr.com/post/175338444821/where-are-we-now-with-hiaps-post-fossil (published 28 June 2018).

Literature

— Bloom, Brett. *Petro Subjectivity: De-industrializing Our Sense of Self.* Auburn (IN): Breakdown Break Down Press, 2015.
— Haraway, Donna. 'Symbiogenesis, Sympoiesis and Art Science Activisms for Staying with the Trouble.' In *Arts of Living on a Damaged Planet*, edited by Anna Lowenhaupt Tsing et al., pp. 25-27, 45. Minneapolis: University of Minnesota Press, 2017.
–. *Staying with the Trouble: Making Kin in the Chthulucene.* London and Durham: Duke University Press, 2016.
— Hildyard, Daisy. *The Second Body.* London: Fitzcarraldo Editions, 2017.
— Parikka, Jussi. 'Cartographies of Environmental Arts.' In *The Midden*, edited by Jenni Nurmenniemi and Tracey Warr, p. 85. Helsinki: Garret Publications, 2018.
— Salminen, Antti, and Tere Vadén. *Energy and Experience: An Essay in Nafthology.* Chicago: MCM Press, 2015.

Residing in Trouble

Antti Majava

Last winter, the Kainuu region in Central Finland was troubled by freezing rain and snowfall intensified by climate change. In the Mustarinda residency we had to survive six days without electricity. Also, part of the time roads were cut off due to the large number of fallen trees. This summer Finland suffered a record drought, which has largely destroyed the crops.

The Arctic is warming twice as fast as the world average. Climate change, pollution, chemicalization, loss of biodiversity and changes in land use accelerate each other's negative effects. We are facing drastic and threatening transformations in our daily lives. Right now.

The Mustarinda Association was founded to promote ecological and cultural diversity and to produce new critical perspectives on the relationship between humans and the environment. We are determined to do our best for a cultural and societal development that is in balance with the load-bearing capacity of the natural systems.

We knew from the beginning that starting an international artist residency in the middle of nowhere, in Hyrynsalmi, would be an ecological paradox. The long flights of residency guests make up the largest source of pollution in our operation. Next in line is heating the facility, followed by food, and transportation in the area.

From the start, our goal was to minimize pollution and we replaced the oil-based heating system of the house with geothermal heat. We also installed a wind turbine and improved the insulation of the house. At present the windmill has been replaced with solar panels and we purchase electricity from a local wind farm. The Mustarinda house has its own back-up power system and a garden. We serve only vegetarian food at our gatherings and public events. An electric car, which is charged mainly with electricity from our solar panel system, is used for transportation in the area. Our emissions have dropped by over 90 per cent.

Emissions from flying pose a more difficult challenge. After lengthy consideration, we decided that the spring 2019 residency programme requires its participants from Europe to travel without flying, taking trains, busses, and boats instead. Residency artists arriving from other continents may fly, but they must pay significant emission compensation. This decision will decrease the climate emissions of transportation in our residency programme by roughly 70 per cent. We follow with interest how the decision will affect the number of applications.

One would expect that the emissions caused by an art residency would drop to a minimum if artists stayed in their hometowns. However, this is not always the case. It has been shown that the infrastructure of cities and urban lifestyles often lead to more consumption than country life. Life in Mustarinda, more than twenty kilometres away from the nearest supermarket, can be less consumptive by virtue of circumstance.

In the best case, residencies can be platforms for experimenting with low-carbon post-fossil ways of living and working and thus promote these in general. It may be easier to adopt new energy technologies, low-emission travelling and a healthy low-carbon diet in a residency than at home. Residencies can also support a change toward sustainability in the norms of the art world.

Cultivation or Culture War

In exceptional unity, the international scientific community agrees that societies must rapidly transform in order to overcome the threats. The art field must also choose whether to support the rapid and extensive transition into sustainability or to prepare for a chaotic collapse of the natural systems. In the latter case, the arts probably won't matter anymore.

Over the last two decades, social-ecological phenomena and environmental politics have only just begun to establish themselves as fields of research. Cultural perspectives on humans-environment relations, ecological objectives, and sustainability are only just taking shape. Societal inability to respond to the urgent crisis has drawn the social, cultural and psychological factors that seem to hinder rational action to the fore of the sustainability sciences.

The arts have the ability to form comprehensive perspectives on human and human-nonhuman relations, which is turning out extremely valuable from a scientific as well as societal viewpoint. On the other hand, overtheorizing may cloud the path towards concrete transformation of our practices.

Because Western societies are built on abstractions of endless growth in economy, production, and consumption, we should be ready for a rapid change in society's operating logic. This cannot take place, however, without a process of re-organization, which requires patience. It is interesting that art has the capacity to question market logic while being a commodity itself. Support for new ways of life and ideals that are not based on consumption and the pursuit of financial gain may be found in the various traditions of art.

Residency programmes operating outside the big cities can have a key role in the fight against culture wars. The polarized divides between advocates for nature conservation and its opponents, between countryside and cities, the educated and uneducated, the rich and poor, believers and nonbelievers pose an increasing threat both to democratic systems and to the environment. Discrimination against rural areas drives their residents to support destructive forces such as Trump. The problem of cities is blindness to Earth's life-supporting systems. A single day without food and other resources produced by the countryside would leave the cities in serious trouble.

The producer price inflation mainly caused by urban consumers is one of the central reasons for rural distress. Unsustainable pricing of production explains why agriculture and forestry are acting as carbon sources instead of carbon sinks. Rural areas enable natural climate solutions, and according to new studies their potential is comparable to the reduction in fossil fuel use. Preventing a political and an environmental catastrophe would require directing attention outside the cities.

Mortal Arts

The present practices of the international art world are far from ecologically sustainable. An average residency artist may be estimated to travel by plane at least five times a year between residencies, exhibition venues, studio, home, and the homes of family and friends.

Both fuel emissions and radiative forcing[1] of the condensation trail of airplanes should be included when counting the emissions of flights. Calculated this way, two intercontinental flights and three flights within Europe have a climatic effect of 20 tons of carbon dioxide. Even if the resident would otherwise attempt to live a low-emission lifestyle (roughly 10,000 kg per year), the total carbon footprint would be around 30,000 kg, in other words, twice the average German citizen, almost six times higher than the world average, and fourteen-fold compared to a sustainable level.

In addition to the environmental problem, the comparison reveals a huge gap in living standards between the art world and the majority of humankind. The consequences of climate change and other effects of overconsumption are estimated to lead to the deaths of millions of people. In Africa alone tens of millions of people have to leave their homes and head to Europe. Emission reductions or their neglection is thus also a major human rights issue.

It is imperative that key art institutions lead the way in structural transition towards sustainability. However, all five of the world's most prestigious contemporary art biennials keep quiet about ecological sustainability factors on their websites.

Current societal commitments and concrete actions will not lead even close to the target of curbing global warming below 2°C. Unfortunately, only a small percentage of the tens of thousands of residencies, museums, galleries, and other art spaces and programmes have taken more progressive actions than official governmental policies require to minimize the ecological footprint of their operation. For example, the new spaces of the Whitney Museum and the expansion plans of Tate Modern are ecologically high-standard. However, neither institution present a concrete plan to curb the largest source of emissions of art professionals and art audience, which is air travel.

The art world has adopted as one of its core principles to promote the mobility of people and goods. The increase in free movement, which is based almost entirely on air travel, is generously supported by EU grants, scholarships and airline tax deductions. It is justified to ask whether the continued increase in mobility is a sensible objective for the arts in the era of climate threat.

Without a doubt, mobility also has positive consequences. However, it is time to evaluate what kind of qualitative factors are linked to mobility. Is all mobility positive or even necessary for the development of the field of art? It is likely that considerable emission reductions can be achieved by reorganizing functions in the art world without anyone even noticing the difference. Yet as the necessary actions have been delayed for decades, we must also be prepared for changes that affect the foundational structures of the arts. Preparing for change in its various aspects should begin immediately.

As it stands, a personal decision to avoid flying may lead to marginalization in the art world. It is clear that individuals alone should not bear the responsibility for change. Institutions must clear the way. Art organizations may think they have invested enough in books, publications, discussions, and theorization dealing with environmental themes. But they have not taken the step from words to action. On the contrary, over-theorization may have even blurred understanding about how their ecological footprint can be concretely reduced.

Sometimes ecological questions and directives are perceived as demands that instrumentalize and restrict artistic freedom. Ecological preconditions are thus identified with economic and political preconditions, which are of course negotiable and reflect prevailing ideals. Ecological preconditions are, however, neither a matter of choice nor are they negotiable. To live in accordance with them is not an ethical or freedom-restricting choice but the only chance for the continuation of life and culture.

Funding shortages and the constant struggle for existence can draw the attention in the arts away from the pursuit of ecological sustainability. It is to be expected that the expense of maintaining the infrastructure and over-consumptive practices will continue to increase. Ecologically sustainable practices are often also the most direct route to long-term economic sustainability.

The Power of Clapping Hands

Dennis Meadows, one of the writers of *The Limits to Growth* report, published in 1972 (a milestone of ecological thinking) gave a good example at the 40th anniversary of the report. He asked the audience to clap their hands, when he said 'clap'. He even emphasized: 'I want you to clap your hands when I say clap hands.' Then Meadows counted to three and clapped his hands and everyone in the audience clapped their hands. Right after that Meadows said 'clap'. In the silence that followed his request, it became clear that nobody acted according to his verbal instructions, but that everyone followed his embodied example. Meadows used his example to explain that speeches and theorizing don't compare with practical examples in societal changes. In residencies, artists and researchers can experience and live out new practices, which are necessary to adopt in order to preserve a societal and cultural continuum similar to the present.

Ecological art,[2] speech and theorizing can give art audiences various interesting perspectives. A catastrophe can only be avoided with good examples, ways of thinking and practices that help to reduce actual emissions and environmental damages.

Post-fossil Reasoning

In many collaborative projects with different organizations Mustarinda develops ways to promote post-fossil and ecological practices in the art world. One of the most important areas of development is the adaptation of energy consumption to the fluctuations of renewable energy production, especially solar and wind energy, which depend on weather conditions.

The adaptation can be eased by different smart grid solutions and by storing energy into water storages and structures of the house. In addition to technological solutions we need to change our way of thinking. This means, for example, accepting a fluctuation of five degrees Celsius in workspace temperature depending on the weather. I am currently working on a study of the effects of temperature fluctuations on working and living experiences in a residency. The study will form a part of my doctoral thesis.

The history of air travel is closely associated with the development of artistic imagination from the Renaissance onwards. Early twentieth-century avantgarde was strongly associated with dreams about techno-utopias enabled by fossil fuels in which almost anything would be possible. For one reason or another, the biospheric preconditions and different dimensions of life in coherence with them have not inspired artists and art audiences as powerfully.

Ultimately, the most fundamental question about the transition to sustainability may be what energy is produced for.[3] The demand for energy in a society at a given time and meeting it are not so much technical or economic questions as cultural and social ones.

The infrastructural requirements of art are often still perceived as a concern distinct from artistic content. The environmental crisis, however, forces us to think of the structures necessary for the arts as inseparable from the artistic content. Thus, for example, the energy solutions of a residency or a gallery are an essential part of their conception of art.

We hope that a journey to Mustarinda would not be about exhausting residency-hopping but one of the most important experiences in the resident's professional and personal life. The residency period begins when the front door at home is closed. The journey by different means of transportation through Europe, the Baltic countries, Scandinavia, and the Baltic Sea is an integral part of the residency experience.

A scheduled flight from Copenhagen to Tokyo flies across the forested lands surrounding Mustarinda every day. It is very likely that none of the passengers are aware of the plane passing over the Mustarinda, Paljakka, or Kainuu region. Species of plants, fungi, animals, humans and various life-supporting systems are hidden within the colour fields formed by forests, swamps, farmlands, and lakes.

Notes

1 Radiative forcing or climate forcing is the difference between insolation (sunlight) absorbed by the Earth and energy radiated back to space (Source: Wikipedia).

2 At a general level the concept of ecology refers to all action and thinking related to environmental factors. Ecology can be interpreted as both the neutral study of environmental relations and a moral imperative to prevent ecological crisis. Therefore, ecological perspectives do not necessarily include solutions for concrete environmental problems. A book or a theory dealing with ecological questions can also, among other things, study ecological relations in the context of global environmental crisis.

3 Shove and Walker 2014.

Literature

- Barnosky, Anthony D., et al. 'Introducing the Scientific Consensus on Maintaining Humanity's Life Support Systems in the 21st Century: Information for Policy Makers.' *The Anthropocene Review* 1, no. 1 (2014). doi: 10.1177/2053019613516290.
- BIOS. *Governance of Economic Transition*. https://bios.fi/bios-governance_of_economic_transition.pdf, accessed 2 October 2018.
- Cumming, Laura. 'Revolution: Russian Art 1917-1932: Review: When Anything Was Possible.' *The Guardian*, 12 February 2017. www.theguardian.com/artanddesign/2017/feb/12/revolution-russian-art-1917-1932-review.
- Griscom, Bronson W., et al. 'Natural Climate Solutions.' *Proceedings of the National Academy of Sciences* 114, no. 44 (October 2017), pp. 11645-11650. doi:10.1073/pnas.1710465114.
- Hoffman, Andrew J. 'Climate Science as Culture War.' *Stanford Social Innovation Review*. (Fall 2012). https://ssir.org/book_reviews/entry/climate_science_as_culture_war, accessed 2 October 2018.
- Järvensivu, Paavo. 'A Post-fossil Fuel Transition Experiment: Exploring Cultural Dimensions from a Practice-theoretical Perspective.' *Journal of Cleaner Production* 169, no. 15 (December 2017, pp. 143-51. doi: 10.1016/j.jclepro.2017.03.154.
- Lodder, Christina. 'Man, Space and the Zero of Form: Kazimir Malevich's Suprematism and Natural World.' In *Meanings of Abstract Art*, edited by Paul Crowther and Isabel Wünche, pp. 47-63. New York: Routledge, 2012.
- Meadows, Dennis. *Perspectives on the Limits of Growth: It is Too Late for Sustainable Development*. Speech in Smithsonian Institute, 3 March 2012. www.youtube.com/watch?v=f2oyU0RusiA, accessed 2 October 2018.
- Missirian, Anouch, and Wolfram Schlenker. 'Asylum Applications Respond to Temperature Fluctuations.' *Science* 358, no. 6370 (December 2017), pp. 1610-14. doi: 10.1126/science.aao0432.
- Ottelin, Juudit, Jukka Heinonen, and Seppo Junnila. 'New Energy Efficient Housing Has Reduced Carbon Footprints in Outer but Not in Inner Urban Areas.' *Environmental Science & Technology* 49 (2015), pp. 9574-83. doi: 10.1021/acs.est.5b02140.
- Rockström, Johan, et al. 'A Roadmap for Rapid Decarbonisation.' *Science* 355, no. 6331 (March 2017), pp. 1269-71. doi: 10.1126/science.aah3443.
- Shove, Elizabeth, and Gordon Walker. 'What Is Energy For? Social Practice and Energy Demand.' *Theory, Culture & Society* 31, no. 5 (1 July 2014), pp. 41-58. doi: 10.1177/0263276414536746.
- WHO. *Climate Change and Health*. www.who.int/news-room/fact-sheets/detail/climate-change-and-health, accessed 2 October 2018.

Cosmopolitics for Retreats

Taru Elfving

> Visiting is not an easy practice; it demands the ability to find others actively interesting ... to cultivate the wild virtue of curiosity, to retune one's ability to sense and respond—and to do all this politely![1]

I am writing this at the end of yet another record-breaking summer. The heat wave and drought have now left their temporary marks in the landscape, yet only time will tell how deep these impacts may become. They add yet another layer onto the rich, entangled sediments of an island off the South-West coast of Finland, where I am currently developing a new residency programme for artists. This hide-away in a vast archipelago appears pristine to an urban eye, yet under the surface of the surrounding Baltic Sea lies a particularly fragile low-salinity marine ecosystem affected by pollution of myriad kinds for decades already. Carefully conserved forests, specific to these very isles, are meanwhile home to another near-invisible threat. Ticks, the disease-carrying tiny bloodsuckers that are fast spreading further North thanks to the warming climate, thrive in the region with their host animals, white-tailed deer. These non-native species of deer, introduced to Finland in the thirties, are now naturalized citizens of the islands and most of the mainland forests with hardly any other predators except human hunters and reckless drivers.

The island of Seili is a microcosm that reflects the acute planetary challenges of the present against complex historical trajectories. Long-term scientific mapping of changes in the local ecosystem entwine here with centuries of institutionalized othering and biopolitics. Since the mid-sixties, the island has been home to the Archipelago Research Institute of Turku University, which holds a unique collection of scientific data. This now provides the basis for interdisciplinary modelling of future impacts of environmental change as well as for analysis of the complex co-dependencies between different species, including humans. Prior to the establishment of the Institute, the island served as a site of confinement for lepers since the early seventeenth century and later as a mental hospital for women. Today, a growing number of tourists flock to the island in the summer months, thanks to the financialization of education that has compelled the university to rent out many of the buildings to a restaurant and hotel business.

This is a rough sketch of the multi-species community and ecosystem that acts as a soundboard for my thinking on residencies here. As a newcomer, and without roots in the area, I may well be considered an invader on the island, not unlike the ticks and the deer or the tourists. Just visiting. The ongoing ecological changes entangled with the history of enforced confinement haunts any consideration of belonging on the island. To be a resident, even a temporary one merely passing through, is never a neutral matter of choice. Rather, it raises myriad questions concerning rights, access, and sustainability. Any ability to take up residence implies a considerable privilege–whether in the field of artist residencies or in other senses of the word. Who can choose to become a temporary resident, and under what terms?

Residency is, after all, never something simply assumed, but rather granted. In artist residencies there is a contract, however informal or without strings attached, that determines certain codes of conduct and mutually agreed upon aims. There is a professional framework that lays down some kind of cornerstones even if the residency is otherwise completely autonomously programmed. Yet, whether, and if so, how this nurtures belonging or intensifies a sense of responsibility as a resident is another question. As on the island of Seili, all residencies are both specifically situated and connected to forces and flows beyond their immediate context. Taking up residence therefore requires assuming accountability for one's engagements locally as well as for all their potentially far-reaching and unpredictable reverberations, which are accelerated in the global circulation and uneven distribution of artists, capital, and effects of climate change today.

This amounts to a formidable challenge that has to be reckoned with in the field of artist residencies rather than ushered solely onto the shoulders of individual practitioners, as I will argue in the following. How can residencies thus cultivate response-abilities in relation to the many facets of the temporary homes they offer, of the environments and communities in their complexity? Or, in the words of Donna Haraway, how to 'hold in regard, to respond, to look back reciprocally, to notice, to pay attention, to have courteous regard for, to esteem: all of that is tied to polite greeting, to constituting the polis, where and when species meet'?[2]

Mobile Residents

One place to start is to look up what the terms related to residencies actually signify. The word 'residence' originates from Latin ('one who remains seated') and refers to the domicile or official residence of a ruler or high official, usually an imposing dwelling such as a castle or manor. On the other hand, the English words 'residence', 'residency' and 'resident' open up a plethora of positions, associations, and related practices: foreign agents in the history of colonialism and espionage, medical students specializing in hospitals, individuals and businesses registered in some location, student housing, teaching positions, and official housing at the workplace. In a more general sense, residence refers to long-term or permanent domicile, or a programme or file residing in the memory of a computer rather than being loaded from somewhere else. It also refers to birds that do not migrate according to the changing seasons.[3]

Birds, however, are unlikely to define their own sense of belonging and residence in this way. The future relationship between computers/artificial intelligence and location, then again, remains to be seen. For people, on the other hand, settling in a place is always somehow finite, temporal and regulated. An examination of the terminology and practices of residences reveals that this anthropocentric perspective and attempt to determine different degrees of attachment to someplace or to something are negotiable, and historically and culturally specific. Yet, these attachments do matter.

In its various significations, therefore, the word residency draws us to the volatile fault lines of the present in between permanence and change, belonging and rootlessness, or local and planetary. The term 'artist residency' strikingly places artists and their work in these very borderlands of unresolved contradictions that open up a rich array of challenges and potentialities. Being a resident is not an opposite to being on the move.

This calls for revisiting the ideas of mobility, especially as an alarming number of people appear to be rather in favour of rebuilding walls today. In addition to the surge in populist politics, the interconnected neoliberal global capitalism and escalating climate crisis increase the challenges faced in this task in complex ways. The age of innocence is over when it comes to international mobility, even within Europe. Mobility has been valued in EU policies on art and culture in the name of intercultural and transnational exchange. During the last two decades, this has been driven simultaneously by idealistic impulses, diplomatic soft power, the realpolitik of building Fortress Europe, and economic interests. The present tendency is to quantify the benefits of mobility– alongside everything else including basic scientific or artistic research—in terms of profit and growth. This adds to the pressure to measure short-term impact, productivity, and applicability, rather than long-term changes and complex patterns of emergence, as many writers in this book argue.

However, while mobility can no longer be embraced uncritically, there is an acute need for ever-stronger arguments for its necessity. But what does it mean to be mobile in times of enforced migrations, reinforced borders, growing xenophobia, an escalating climate crisis, and mass extinctions? Who has access to global circulation? How and in what processes of value production does mobility take part? Who and what are actually served by travel and, for example, 'networking'? What is the cost of being on the move—ecologically, socially, personally, intellectually?

Entangled Ecologies

'It is not only species that are becoming extinct but also the words, phrases, and gestures of human solidarity.'[4]

Sustainability of travel needs to be addressed today in broader terms than carbon footprint. In order to make sense of the potential and challenges of mobility in the arts today, it is necessary to reflect on how ecological questions, as well as cultural and knowledge production, are interconnected with economy and geopolitics. The work of art professionals is entangled in this web in numerous ways. As recent political events have made clear, there are undeniable connections between neoliberal austerity politics, growing inequality, and the rise of populist nationalism. But this also unveils the legacies of colonialism in global capitalism and the interrelations between racism, sexism, and 'extractivism'—the instrumentalized approach to both natural and human resources.[5] How the financialization of culture and the new forms of precarity entwine with all of this, concerns us in the arts deeply.

Who can travel? Who can choose to not travel? For what reasons, by what means, at what cost? This all has to do with access—to movement across geopolitical borders, to material resources as well as knowledge and discourse, to funds and support structures, to time and space. The increasing inequality of access has become obvious also within Europe, but it is amplified manifold in the global circulation. Therefore, the calls for intersectional solidarity between various histories and forms of oppression, and for awareness of their interconnections, are urgent within the arts today.

Félix Guattari's call for a transversal understanding of ecology remains highly relevant here: 'Now more than ever, nature cannot be separated from culture; in order to comprehend the interactions between ecosystems, the mechanosphere and the social and individual Universes of reference, we must learn to think "transversally".'[6] The three entwined ecological registers defined by Guattari–the environment, the social, and the mental–all need to be addressed in order to consider the complex interrelated processes and impacts of the arts: how do the knowledge and value produced in and through the practices in the arts reinforce or challenge the unsustainable structures that permeate society today? What processes do these practices participate in or contribute to–in terms of their environmental impacts, but also power relations in their communities and modes of communication, and in terms of their subjective affects?

This requires consideration of both the infrastructures and values powering and conditioning our practices and subjectivities, from funding models, modes of travel, sources of energy and food consumed to organizational structures or terms of inclusion and exclusion. What kind of alternatives to growth-based economies can be nurtured in the residencies? Or, what kind of models of non-hierarchical decision making can be experimented with? What does radical hospitality imply in practice today? For example, what does it mean to state in the context of international contemporary art, as the Mayor of Palermo does: 'Here in Palermo ... there are no migrants. Those who arrive in the city become Palermitans'?[7]

How to, furthermore, navigate within the contradiction lived in residencies today between surviving in the accelerated project and attention economy, on the one hand, and the aim to offer retreats, on the other? What does it take to live up to the promise of residencies as retreats from the pressures of production and even of political persecution? Or, as retreats for artistic development rather than mere networking and cv-building? Or, for cross-cultural dialogue or interdisciplinary collaborations rather than site-specific-lite productions for global circulation that exhaust local communities as resources?

Retreats in Transition

The very term retreat may then be another good place to pause at. By definition, retreat refers to an act of withdrawing from what is difficult, dangerous, or disagreeable; a process of receding from a position or state attained; a place of privacy or safety; and a period of group withdrawal for prayer, meditation, or study. Retreat refers thus to a place and a time but also to movement. In resonant terms residencies can be often understood as intense experiences of isolation and (self)reflection, but also in terms of transitions as well as immersions in novel contexts and communities. All kinds of critical encounters take place in residencies as retreats.

Residencies can be seen as active sites of transformation and artists-in-residence as mediators who move between and connect places and people, cultural contexts, site-specific and disciplinary knowledges, subjective and shared experiences. They gather and disseminate ideas and methods. They are challenged and influenced, while they also challenge and influence others, both in everyday and in professional interactions. They weave connections between the local and the planetary, both in their work and in their interrelations. While residencies appear as nodes on a map of transnational circulation, they are always also specific sites, where the so-called site-specificity has to be critically re-considered. In the era of advanced globalization and climate change, each and every site is already deeply embedded in planetary processes. Their specificities only come into focus in and through relations to elsewhere. Site-specificity is thus relational yet non-scalable, resistant to universalizing applications.[8] Moreover, site can be understood as a situation, an event. It is not a backdrop, an object of study, or an environment to inhabit–rather, it is in ceaseless formation that we are all part of. In residencies, as on an island, the relations within and beyond intensify, demanding heightened awareness of what is brought, left behind, and taken away. Retreat as a total withdrawal is a dangerous illusion.

Sensitivity to local particularities requires critical positioning of the artist, curator, or researcher engaging with it in the midst of the ongoing movement between places. Who and what do these engagements serve? Can they have any local impact or global effects beyond the value production in the sphere of the international art world? The circulation of people in residencies does not necessarily differ so much from the circulation of art works among the institutions, biennales, and art fairs. At best this mobility allows for acknowledgement of historical, present, or emergent connections across the globe. But at worst the practices and the works lose their capacity to communicate the subtle yet significant differences and feed into the simplified, monolithic visions of the world framed by the global market. When people move and meet other people, all kinds of transformative encounters are indeed possible, but not guaranteed.

How and when do residencies truly allow for commitment to critical reflection and openness for unexpected entanglements, or for research and experimentation without predefined ends? As different contributions to this book attest to, retreat does not always involve considerable distances. Some residencies locally offer alternative platforms as well as longer-term support structures in response to the needs of precarious artists and practices that do not fit into the project economy or the market. Meanwhile, it is paramount to acknowledge the diverse drivers behind travel. Voluntary mobility is not an option for everyone, as in the case of artists under political threat, for whom the temporary space-time for concentration is as invaluable as the integration into professional artistic communities that residencies can provide. For others, then again, residencies in remote non-urban sites allow for momentary withdrawal from battles focused on environmental concerns, where they can recharge and re-ground, reflect on their practice, and contribute to a community of shared sensibilities. Residencies may also be positively exclusive, such as in the case of residencies fostering sharing amongst, for example, indigenous artistic practices and knowledge.

Residencies can thus function as safe spaces in radically different ways. As retreats they are then crucially not detached but rather 'connected', plugged into the (art) world and, furthermore, its various communities, not only via communications technologies but also through the specific networks and programmes of the residencies in question.[9] Here the response-ability of residency organizations comes to the fore: how do they situate themselves and articulate their specific critical as well as practical frameworks that determine not only the operations of the organization but also what they offer to and expect of the residents? How do they work against individualistic competition and accelerated production while nurturing sustainable choices alongside experimentation, collectivity as well as complexity?

Future Cosmopolitics

> The problem is not with attachment; the problem may be that some of us, those who call themselves 'moderns',

> confuse their attachments with universal obligations, and thus feel free to define themselves as 'nomads', free to go everywhere, to enter any practical territory, to judge, deconstruct or disqualify what appears to them as illusions or folkloric beliefs and claims.[10]

Reflection on the role of residencies today requires rethinking cosmopolitanism and the related universalizing ideals of global citizenry with its troubling colonial legacy and anthropocentrism. I propose here a shift of emphasis from cosmopolitanism to cosmopolitics, as resonant with residencies when understood as 'calling for the invention of modes of gathering that complicate politics by introducing hesitation', following Isabelle Stengers.[11]

However, re-consideration of cosmopolitanism remains important in the wider context of the international art world that residencies are an integral part of. Writing on 'aesthetic cosmopolitanism', Nikos Papastergiadis has focused on the significance of globally oriented contemporary art practices and their relationship to transnational social movements. He argues that a diverse range of locally rooted artistic practices today demonstrate a shared consciousness towards global issues, yet they cannot be grouped together based on formal resemblances or on common cultural traditions. These practices can provide new grounding for the debates on the politics of globalization, the ethics of hospitality, and the culture of cosmopolitanism, as they create alternative models for cross-cultural dialogue.[12]

'Art has a role in both forging a specific knowledge of the world and initiating new modes of being in the world', Papastergiadis writes, and continues that art has a capacity 'not only to capture a cosmopolitan vision of the world but also to initiate situations in which the artists and public participants are engaged in the mediation of new forms of cosmopolitan agency.'[13] The promise of knowledge, visions, modes of being and forms of agency are not easy to deliver. Rather, the challenge of cosmopolitanism is that it requires radical openness and recognition of irreducible differences. This resonates with the notion of cosmopolitics proposed by Stengers, which calls for decisions to be made in the presence of all those affected. This attentiveness disallows for 'any shortcut or oversimplification, any a priori differentiation between that which counts and that which does not'.[14] Moreover, it allows for the expansion of the notion of community and the ethics of co-dependence beyond humans. There are no quick fixes here, no universal solutions, transcendent common interests, or mutual understandings.

Cosmopolitics cannot therefore be programmatic.[15] It is rather a matter of practice. Or, in Rosi Braidotti's words, it is 'a *praxis* (a grounded shared project), not a *doxa* (a common-sense belief)'.[16] Furthermore, it requires slowing down, which is easier in theory than in practice amidst the project and attention economy, as residencies can attest to. It may also seem deeply problematic in the face of the urgencies and multiple crises unfolding at a terrifying pace. Yet it appears undeniably necessary, especially in the field of the arts and critical thought, to situate one's practice(s): to reflect on and to articulate what means and aims, affiliations and attachments guide one's practice and how.

Cosmopolitical practice opens up thus from within one's own tradition of thought and reaches outward towards thinking and sharing with others.[17] As T.J. Demos reminds the Western reader, cosmopolitical world views have a long-standing history in indigenous cultures, which has to be acknowledged in any such practice.[18] Cosmopolitics can then become a decolonial, ecological practice that recognizes the economic, gendered, racialized and other power relations at play. This intersectionalist politics of aesthetics Demos calls for is attentive to the interaction between local activities and global formations, and is often nurtured in interdisciplinary collaborations.[19]

Residencies may well offer great platforms for these emergent practices and experiments with cosmopolitics, yet this requires critically situated practices–and not just of the artists but also of curators and others working in and shaping the institutions of art.

Emergencies

'Living in a time of planetary catastrophe thus begins with a practice at once humble and difficult: noticing the worlds around us.'[20]

Noticing, in a cosmopolitical sense, requires diverse modes of observation and attentiveness, ranging from artistic and scientific to vernacular and indigenous knowledge practices.[21] Could residencies provide retreats for this epistemological and methodological multiplicity, not unlike the refugia for biodiversity called for by Anna Tsing?[22] Here curiosity may be re-valued and nurtured not as a drive to capture, but rather as an urge to know more that is aligned with care.

Curiosity may well kill the cat, but as Stengers argues, 'relation-making does not consist simply in the recognition that we are related'—rather, it is an achievement that involves a risk of failure.[23] The curious is drawn ever deeper into entanglements of all kinds, never left untouched. These complex inter- and intra-relations have inescapable significance, as anyone affected gutturally by travel knows. Mobility brings with it potential contagions ranging from intellectual to bacterial.

Could nomadism within the context of artist residencies be therefore rethought and rehearsed as a situated, relational practice rather than individualistic residency hopping of a citizen of everywhere and nowhere?[24] Yet, why should this involve any further travel? After all, globalization has opened up networks that allow for new modes of exchange, global resistance and movement building to take place. Can travel still work against the formation of detached bubbles and populist polarizations that those very same online media and platforms have nurtured?

The rhetoric around mobility of invasive species on the one hand and immigration on the other, continue to resonate with each other to an ever more alarming effect. This demands acute examination and experimentation with alternative experiences, understandings, and languages of transformation. Residencies offer particular space-times for this urgently needed work that requires commitment and care. Rather than feeding paralyzing apocalyptic doomsday scenarios they may also nurture a future-oriented search for hope amidst forces of change and related processes of emergence.[25]

Ecological awareness at this time of climate change requires that planetary perspectives are also grounded and responsive to the irreducible specificities of local, ever-changing ecosystems. Here further knowledge and access to information is not enough for the needed transition, as many frustrated climate scientists are saying today. As retreats, residencies may act as laboratories for situating and re-grounding ourselves in this turmoil—with a focus not only on what but also on how to practice—as artists, curators, institutions. International artist residencies can offer safe spaces for hospitality, generosity and sharing rather than ever-increasing competition for survival. They also raise the question of what it means to be offered temporary residence today. This comes with promises, possibilities and responsibilities. Being a resident cannot be the same as being a tourist consuming novel experiences and environments, or an explorer in search of new resources to extract, or an introvert hermit momentarily retreating to wherever elsewhere.

Travel may not always involve long geographical distances—such as in the case of specifically focused residencies, or those outside of the art context and hosted by universities, community initiatives, or even businesses. Retreat can be a withdrawal from some kind of action and interaction, but simultaneously a dynamic activation of other modes of engagements and sensibilities: not necessarily literally retreating from the centre—from cities or structures of the art world—but radically challenging the very notion of the centre through retreat from traditions of thought or habitual patterns of practice.

Retreat may also mean withdrawal from the battles of boundary-making between, for example, forms of knowledge. It may imply withholding judgement and rather listening attentively, even for a moment, and feeling the edges of the different practices in question.[26] Slowing down can then actually be an acceleration of our critical and creative capacities of response-ability. It calls for experiments with forms and formulations of community, collectivity, and co-existence that work to break with institutional hierarchies as well as all gendered, racialized, and naturalized power dynamics. To support this, institutions have to become accountable for their blind spots and exclusions. They need to commit to the development of practices across those borders that are being reinforced right now—between cultures and peoples, between disciplines and modes of knowledge, and between individual practices and collective processes.

Meanwhile the sense of emergency should not lead to a fear or dismissal of complexity and opacity. Rather, with an acute awareness of the always partial positions and perspectives, the insistence on the diversity of epistemologies does not have to add up to post-factual relativism.[27] Quite the contrary, to take time to do the necessary hard work of situating our practices in the face of the multiple intertwined urgencies today can allow us to challenge the competing bubbles of alternative facts. This requires acknowledgement of the heterogeneity of time and space unsettling the coordinates of every temporary resident and island retreat.

Notes

1 Haraway 2016, p. 127. Haraway, furthermore, here references Hannah Arendt's thought on training imagination to go visiting, and Vinciane Despret on politeness as an epistemological position and practice. Arendt 1982; Despret 2005.
2 Haraway 2008, p. 19.
3 See e.g. Oxford Dictionaries (en.oxforddictionaries.com) and Merriam-Webster (www.merriam-webster.com) online.
4 Guattari 2000, p. 29.
5 See e.g. Klein 2014.
6 Guattari 2000, p. 29.
7 Orlando 2018, p. 9.
8 See Anna Tsing on site-specificity and non-scalability. Tsing 2015.
9 Martini and Michelkevičius 2013, p. 11.
10 Stengers 2005, p. 191.
11 Stengers 2018, p. 151.
12 Papastergiadis 2012.
13 Ibid., p. 11.
14 Stengers 2018, p. 152.
15 Ibid., p. 151.
16 Braidotti 2013, pp. 92-93.
17 Stengers 2018, p. 156.
18 Demos 2016, p. 23.
19 Ibid., p. 12-13.
20 Tsing et al. 2017, p. M7.
21 Ibid.
22 Tsing 2015.
23 Stengers 2018, p. 146.
24 See Rosi Braidotti's notion of nomadic subject, e.g. in relation to the question of practice. Braidotti 2013, pp. 92-93.
25 See e.g. Kirksey 2015.
26 Stengers 2005, p. 184.
27 My emphasis on epistemological multiplicity, or discourse-diversity as termed by Tracey Warr, arises out of the project *Frontiers in Retreat* I initiated at HIAP Helsinki International Artist Programme (2013-2018). For an elaborated discussion see: Elfving 2018.

Literature

- Arendt, Hannah. *Lectures on Kant's Political Philosophy*, edited by Ronald Beiner Brighton: Harvester Press, 1982.
- Braidotti, Rosi. *The Posthuman.* Cambridge, MA: Polity Press, 2013.
- Demos, T.J. *Decolonizing Nature: Contemporary Art and the Politics of Ecology.* Berlin: Sternberg, 2016.
- Despret, Vinciane. 'Sheep Do Have Opinions.' In *Making Things Public: Atmospheres of Democracy*, edited by Bruno Latour and Peter Weibel, pp. 360–70. Cambridge MA: MIT Press, 2005.
- Elfving, Taru. 'How to Retreat to the Frontiers.' In *The Midden: Frontiers in Retreat*, edited by Jenni Nurmenniemi and Tracey Warr. Helsinki: Garret Publications, 2018.
- Guattari, Félix. *The Three Ecologies.* London and New Brunswick, NJ: Athlone Press, 2000.
- Haraway, Donna. *Staying with the Trouble: Making Kin in the Chthulucene.* Durham and London: Duke University Press, 2016.
- Haraway, Donna. *When Species Meet.* Minneapolis: University of Minnesota Press, 2008.
- Kirksey, Eben. *Emergent Ecologies.* Durham and London: Duke University Press, 2015.
- Klein, Naomi. *This Changes Everything: Capitalism vs the Climate.* New York: Simon & Schuster, 2014.
- Martini, Federica, and Vytautas Michelkevičius, eds. *Tourists Like Us: Critical Tourism and Contemporary Art.* Vilnius: Vilnius Academy of Arts Press/Sierre: ECAV, 2013.
- Orlando, Leoluca. 'The City of Palermo and Manifesta 12: A Shared Project.' In *Manifesta 12: The Planetary Garden: Cultivating Coexistence: The European Nomadic Biennial*, edited by Walter Mariotti, pp. 8–9. Milan: Domus, 2018.
- Papastergiadis, Nikos. *Cosmopolitanism and Culture.* Cambridge: Polity Press, 2012.
- Stengers, Isabelle. *Another Science is Possible: A Manifesto for Slow Science.* Cambridge, MA: Wiley, 2018.

  –. 'Introductory Notes on an Ecology of Practices.' *Cultural Studies Review* 11, no. 1. (March 2005), pp. 183–96.
- Tsing, Anna, et al., eds. *Arts of Living on a Damaged Planet: Ghosts and Monsters of the Anthropocene.* Minneapolis: University of Minnesota Press, 2017.
- Tsing, Anna. *The Mushroom at the End of the World: On the Possibility of Life in Capitalist Ruins.* Princeton: Princeton University Press, 2015.

Contributors

Livia Alexander is a curator, writer, and Chair of the Department of Art and Design at Montclair State University (NJ, USA). Her work is focused on examining the relationship between art infrastructure and artistic production, urbanity, cultural politics of food and art, and contemporary art from the Middle East and Southeast Asia. She has curated and directed numerous art and film programmes, exhibitions, and events at renown venues world-wide, most recently 'Unleashing', an extensive site-specific exhibition spanning four buildings at Teachers College, Columbia University. Her award-winning scholarly writing has appeared in the *Journal of Visual Anthropology*, *Framework*, *MERIP*, and as book chapters and catalogue essays. She regularly contributes to *Hyeprallergic*, *Harper's Bazaar Art Arabia*, and *Art Africa*, and founded the online publication ArteEast Quarterly.

Nathalie Anglès is co-founder and Executive Director of Residency Unlimited (RU). Nathalie studied history and political science and is a graduate of the École du MAGASIN international curatorial studies programme in Grenoble, (CNAC-Le Magasin-Grenoble France). From 2000-2008 she worked at Location One as the Director of the International Residency Program (New York). Previous positions include: Sotheby's (London), cataloguer Impressionist and Modern Art Department; Director of the Residency Program, American Center in Paris; curatorial assistant, École nationale supérieure des Beaux-Arts (ENSBA), Paris; curatorial assistant, Union centrale des Arts Décoratifs (UCAD), Paris. In 2008, Nathalie received the title of Chevalier of the Order of Arts and Letters from the French government.

Helmut Batista lives and works in Rio de Janeiro, Brazil. Batista studied Opera and lived in Europe from 1983 to 1997. He worked as an artist until 1997 and exhibited widely: in Air de Paris (Paris), Massimo De Carlo (Milan), Schipper & Krome (Berlin), Ars Futura (Zurich) and many other places. In 1997 he founded Capacete in Rio de Janeiro as a production agency and a research residency programme, which he directed until 2017. That same year he gave up his post as director and is now working in rethinking new models for independent spaces in South America.

Curator and writer **Taru Elfving** is currently developing an artist residency at the Archipelago Research Institute of Turku University, prior to which she directed the programmes of Frame and HIAP in Helsinki, Finland. Her curatorial work includes 'Hours, Years, Aeons' (Finnish Pavilion, Venice Biennale, 2015), 'Frontiers in Retreat' (HIAP 2013–2018), 'Contemporary Art Archipelago CAA' (Turku 2011, European Capital of Culture), and 'Towards a Future Present' (Lofoten International Art Festival 2008). Elfving has published an extensive body of writing and co-edited publications such as *Altern Ecologies* (Frame, 2016) and the first Finnish anthology on curating *Kuratointi* (Taide, 2017). She holds a PhD from Goldsmiths University of London (2009) and continues to lecture as well as supervise artistic research doctoral students, at the University of the Arts Helsinki and elsewhere.

Pascal Gielen is Full Professor of Sociology of Art and Politics at the Antwerp Research Institute for the Arts (Antwerp University), where he leads the Culture Commons Quest Office (CCQO). Gielen is editor-in-chief of the international book series Arts in Society. In 2016, he became laureate of the Odysseus grant for excellent international scientific research of the Fund for Scientific Research Flanders in Belgium. His research focuses on creative labour, the institutional context of the arts and cultural politics. Gielen has published many books, which have been translated in English, Korean, Polish, Portuguese, Russian, Spanish, and Turkish.

Francisco Guevara is a visual artist, Co-Founder and Co-Director of the Arquetopia Foundation. He specializes in Levinasian ethics applied to the design of transcultural artistic projects and the analysis of performativity in contemporary art practices. His experience spans nearly twenty years of designing, curating, and managing art projects through visual arts education and historiography of art, facilitating Development, sustainability and social transformation. As a visual artist, Guevara investigates the historical construction of the differentiation process and its relationship with the performativity of identity, including gender, class, and race. Guevara received his title of Expert in Management and Planning of Development Aid Projects in the Fields of

Education, Science and Culture from UNED, OEI and CIDEAL, a postgraduate degree in Cultural Management and Communication from FLACSO, and studied Race, Gender and the Historiographies of Art at the University of New Mexico.

Maria Hirvi-Ijäs works as Senior Researcher at the Center for Cultural Policy Research Cupore in Helsinki. She earned her doctoral degree in art research at the University of Helsinki and has held expert positions in the field of art museums and higher art education in Finland and Sweden. As an art researcher her interests are in knowledge production and the societal dimensions of contemporary art. As a cultural policy researcher, she is interested in the politics of culture and the critique of cultural policy.

Jean-Baptiste Joly studied German literature and language in Paris and Berlin. He is a former director of the French Cultural Institute in Stuttgart (1983–1988). From 1989 to 2018 he was CEO of the foundation Akademie Schloss Solitude as founding director and artistic director of the Akademie. Honorary Professor at the Weißensee Kunsthochschule, College of Art and Design, Berlin. Member of the board of trustees of various foundations and cultural institutions in Germany and France. Member of the advisory board of Transcultural Exchange, Boston. Former member (2009–2015) of the French-German Council for Culture.

Patricia Jozef is a Belgian writer. She graduated in Philosophy at the University of Brussels and in Painting at LUCA School of Arts in Ghent. She worked as a researcher at the Museum of Contemporary Art Antwerp (M HKA), at the University of Antwerp, and as a coordinator at the Royal Academy of Fine Arts Antwerp. Her novel *Glory* (2017) focuses on art and philosophy and on the question of who we are and what remains when our professional identity disappears. She is currently teaching Dutch to migrants and refugees and is writing her next novel. Jozef lives and works in Antwerp.

Irmeli Kokko is curator, producer, and educator based in Helsinki. In 1998 she initiated the HIAP–Helsinki International Artist Programme and worked there as director, chairman, and member of the board (1998–2015). She has started residency partnership programmes for Finnish artists at The Frame and at the Academy of Fine Arts she initiated a postgraduate residency programme, supported by the Saastamoinen Foundation. She was a board member of the Res Artis (1999–2001) and expert-group member of residencies at the Arts Council of Finland (1995–2010) and at the Nordic Council of Ministers (2007–2011). As a teacher and lecturer at the Academy of Fine Arts (2006–2018) she conceived the Artist in Society studies that reflects artistic work in relation to the artworld practices and societal changes. She has curated alone and collaboratively several seminars and symposiums. She holds an MA in cultural politics and art education, University of Jyväskylä.

Donna Lynas has been Director of Wysing Arts Centre since 2005 and has developed Wysing's identity as a research centre for the visual arts; introducing experimental artist residencies and retreats, shaping the centre's work in relation to current political and social concerns, developing regional, national, and international partnerships, and commissioning and curating ambitious exhibitions and projects. She established Wysing's critically acclaimed annual festival of art and music in 2010, and developed a music recording studio on Wysing's site with its own record label. Whilst at Wysing, Lynas has worked on new commissions and exhibitions with a large number of artists, including Ed Atkins, Jesse Darling, Michael Dean, Harold Offeh, Imran Perretta, Florence Peake, Elizabeth Price, Laure Prouvost, James Richards and Tai Shani.

Antti Majava is an artist working in multiple medias including installation, light works, photography, video, painting and writing. His main topics are the different aspects of human-nature and art-economy relationships. Majava works in Hyrynsalmi and Helsinki, Finland. He received his MFA from the Finnish Academy of Fine Arts Helsinki in 2008 and is working for a PhD at the Faculty of Arts/Doctoral programme in interdisciplinary environmental sciences at the University of Helsinki. Antti Majava is a co-founder of the Mustarinda Association and BIOS-Research Unit.

Vytautas Michelkevičius (based in Vilnius and Nida, Lithuania) is a curator, researcher, and associate professor whose focus has gradually shifted from photography in the expanded field to media art & theory and lately to artistic research in academia and beyond. He is teaching art practice BA, MA and DA students in Vilnius Academy of Arts and serves as artistic director of Nida Art Colony (2010–2019). He is a member of the Society of Artistic Research (SAR) and a member of the scientific editorial board of peer-reviewed journal *Acoustic Space* (RIXC and Liepaja University, Latvia). He has curated exhibitions related to residencies and artistic research in various situations, among them the Lithuanian Pavilion at the Venice Biennale in 2015. He has edited and co-authored more than ten books on art and media theory and practice.

Nina Möntmann is an art historian, curator', and writer. She is currently Professor of Art Theory at the University of Cologne. Before she has been Professor of Art Theory and the History of Ideas at the Royal Institute of Art in Stockholm, and curator at NIFCA, the Nordic Institute for Contemporary Art in Helsinki. Recent exhibitions include: 'Fluidity' (2016); 'Harun Farocki: A New Product' (2012); 'If we can't get it together: Artists rethinking the (mal)functions of community' (2008); 'The Jerusalem Show: Jerusalem Syndrome' (co-curated with Jack Persekian), 2009; the Armenian Pavillion for the 52nd Venice Biennale (2007). Recent publications include *Kunst als Sozialer Raum* (2002/2017); and the edited volumes *Brave New Work: A Reader on Harun Farocki's film 'A New Product'* (2014); *Scandalous: A Reader on Art & Ethics* (Berlin: Sternberg Press, 2013); *New Communities* (2009) and *Art and Its Institutions* (2006).

Marita Muukkonen, Co-Founding Co-Director of Perpetuum Mobile (PM), is an internationally active curator based in Helsinki. She has been Chairperson of HIAP–The Helsinki International Artists-in-Residence Programme; Curator at HIAP; Curator at FRAME–Contemporary Art Finland; Editor of *FRAMEWORK, The Finnish Art Review*. She has held key functions at NIFCA–The Nordic Institute for Contemporary Art over several years. She has curated and produced exhibitions and projects internationally, in museums such as MoMA in New York, Moderna Museet in Sweden, Kiasma in Finland, and in galleries such as Momentum Gallery in Berlin and Galleri Bo Bjerggaard in Copenhagen. Marita is also a contributor to art journals, catalogues and publications, as well as a regular speaker at international seminars and conferences. Currently, she is developing the large-scale international thematic Re-Aligned Project with its associated multi-disciplinary residency programmes, now in its sixth year. It has included exhibitions, conferences, research, and events in Helsinki, Berlin, Moscow, Tromso, Arkhangelsk, Murmansk, Yekaterinburg, Moscow, and Cairo.

Jenni Nurmenniemi is a Helsinki-based curator. Since 2012, she has worked with HIAP-Helsinki International Artist Programme, where she has been focusing on the intersections of art and ecology, first with the project Frontiers in Retreat: Multidisciplinary Approaches to Ecology in Contemporary Art (2013–2018) and currently with Post-Fossil Transition Project (2018–2020). Her most recent exhibition 'Fictional Frictions', as part of the Gwangju Biennale 2018 Pavilion Project, explores how human life is dependent on other forms of life and complex material processes.

Bojana Panevska is an artist, researcher, and writer; she holds a Bachelor's degree in Audio and Visual Art from the Gerrit Rietveld Academie and a Master's degree in Fine arts from the Sandberg Institute. Her work deals primarily with the physical presence, the online absence and the socio-political-religious consequences of the same. In addition to her artistic practice, she currently manages international collaborations and education, and also facilitates workshops for DutchCulture|TransArtists. Additionally, since 2015, Bojana is the managing editor of TransArtists.org

Alan Quireyns is artistic director of AIR Antwerpen, curator, and writer. He studied art history at the Ghent University and the Freie Universität Berlin and participated in De Appel Curatorial Programme 2009–2010. In his practice, he focuses on the relationship between artistic practices and the everyday. Recent exhibitions include: 'The Living Room XL' (BODEM, Antwerp, 2017); 'Staat van de Stad/State of the City/Zustand der Stadt' (basis e.v., Frankfurt am Main, 2016); 'AIR Traces: Austruweel' (AIR Antwerpen, 2014); 'New Ways to Work' (Extra City Kunsthal, Antwerp, 2012); Recent publications include *The Cabinet of Traces* (2018); *L.A. Magazine* (Espace 251 Nord & AIR

Antwerpen, 2017). Recent texts include: 'Reprobus' (2017); 'Snake Weather', *LA Magazine* (2017); 'Two Fours and One Eight' (2017); 'Persona' (2017); 'The Temporary Inhabitant' (2016); 'The Hand' (2016); 'Bus nr 720' (2016). Alan Quireyns lives and works in Antwerp.

Florian Schneider is the Head of the Trondheim Academy of Fine Art at the Norwegian University of Science and Technology (NTNU) where he currently runs the pilot project 'Art and Ocean', which brings together artists and scientists to explore the potential of new forms of collaborations. Together with Irit Rogoff, he has recently initiated the European Forum for Advanced Practices (EFAP), an independent gathering of artistic and practice-based researchers from across Europe. From 2014 to 2017 he has developed and led the artistic research project 'Divisions' funded by the Norwegian Programme for Artistic Research (PKU). He defended his PhD thesis on 'Imaginary Property' at the Centre for Research Architecture at Goldsmiths College, University of London. Educated as a documentary filmmaker he has written, lectured, produced, exhibited, curated, and collaborated across a wide range of media, fields, disciplines and in independent as well as institutional contexts.

Ivor Stodolsky is Co-Founding Director and Curator of Perpetuum Mobile and an internationally active curator, writer, and theorist. He received a joint honours degree in Philosophy and Mathematics at Bristol University and completed his MRes at the London Consortium (Birkbeck, Tate, BFI, ICA). His doctoral research at Helsinki University was centred on the Russian cultural underground of the eighties and nineties. During his time in academia, he was a CIMo and Ehrenrooth Fellow and worked for several years at the Alexander Institute, London. Prior to this, he worked in global media as Associate Editor of Project Syndicate, 'The World's Opinion Page'. Earlier he co-founded alternative art projects and spaces in London, Vienna, and St. Petersburg. Today, in addition to curating and institution-building, Ivor is an editor and contributor to journals and publications and a speaker on art, politics, and philosophy.

Antennae-
Arts in Society
Book Series

Antennae-Arts in Society Series

Antennae-Arts in Society is a peer-reviewed book series that validates artistic, critical, speculative and essayistic writing as a full academic publishing method. Contributions to the series look upon the arts as 'antennae', feelers for the cultural interpretation and articulation of topical political, economic, social, technological or environmental issues.

The books in this series bring together audiences of diverse backgrounds: artists and other creative makers, academics and researchers from various disciplines, critics, writers, journalists, politicians, curators, and institutional parties, who wish to broaden their view in different political, social and other contexts.

Proposals for book concepts in all artistic and scientific disciplines that take culture as the base of interpretation for the social fabric of our contemporary lives are welcomed and will be considered for publication by the academic board.

Academy of Fine Arts, Helsinki

University of the Arts Helsinki's Academy of Fine Arts

The University of the Arts Helsinki's Academy of Fine Arts offers art studies in Moving Image, Painting, Photography, Printmaking, Site- and Situation-specific Art, and Sculpture as well as Doctoral studies. The Academy is a pioneer in artistic research and has trained artists since 1848. Since 2015, the Academy runs a postgraduate residence programme offering residencies for Finnish artists abroad and a resident fellow programme for artists invited to Finland. The latter provides an opportunity for international artists, researchers, and curators to concentrate on their own projects during a 3-month period. The programme is funded by the Saastamoinen foundation.

www.uniarts.fi

Frame

Frame Contemporary Art Finland

Frame Contemporary Art Finland is an advocate for Finnish contemporary art. Frame supports and promotes international projects, facilitates professional partnerships, and also acts as an information centre for Finnish contemporary art. Frame coordinates Finland's participation in the Venice Biennale.

frame-finland.fi

Index

Colophon

This book is the result of extensive research supported by a series of symposia, seminars, and meetings held between 2015 and 2018. The editors thank all the organizers and participants of the 'Summer Wells' in 2015 and 2018 at the Saari Residence by Kone Foundation, and the symposium 'Residencies Reflected'at HIAP Suomenlinna in 2016, co-organized by HIAP Helsinki International Artist Programme, Academy of Fine Arts and Frame Contemporary Art Finland with the support of Kone Foundation. We want to acknowledge also the value of the symposium 'Reconstructing Rurality' by Rejmyre Art Lab and Nida Art Colony in 2017, and the Res Artis Meetings in Copenhagen 2017 and Rovaniemi 2018, as well as the discourse developed by A-I-R Laboratory CCA Ujazdowski Castle, Fare and Mapping Residencies.

The editors like to express their deepest gratitude to all the individuals whose support has been of vital importance in the editorial process, including Juha Huuskonen at HIAP, Markus Konttinen at the Academy of Fine Arts, Raija Koli at Frame, Marie Fol at TranArtists, DutchCulture, and Mario Caro, Leah O'Loughlin and Leena Vuotovesi at Res Artis. Warmest thanks to the following interviewees, whose insights were invaluable to our research: artists Syowia Kyambi, Tuomas A. Laitinen, Meri Linna and Maria Pääkkönen, Johan Pousette at Iaspis, Leah O'Loughlin at Acme, Danielle Olsen at Wellcome Collection, Jean-Baptiste Joly at Schloss Solitude, Oliver Hickmet at Space, Bojana Panevska and Heidi Vogels at TransArtists, and Nina Möntmann. Last but not least, sincere thanks to all the contributors, who found the time to discuss and share their knowledge amidst the ceaseless everyday labour, struggles, and joy involved in running artist residencies.

Colophon

Contemporary Art Residencies
Reclaiming Time and Space

Editors
Taru Elfving, Irmeli Kokko,
Pascal Gielen

Contributors
Livia Alexander
Nathalie Anglès
Helmut Batista
Taru Elfving
Pascal Gielen
Francisco Guevara
Maria Hirvi-Ijäs
Jean-Baptiste Joly
Patricia Jozef
Irmeli Kokko
Donna Lynas
Antti Majava
Vytautas Michelkevičius
Nina Möntmann
Marita Muukkonen
Jenni Nurmenniemi
Bojana Panevska
Alan Quireyns
Florian Schneider
Ivor Stodolsky

Antennae-Arts *in* Society Series n°27
by Valiz, Amsterdam

Translation
Leo Reijnen

Copy Editing
Leo Reijnen, Els Brinkman

Proofreading
Els Brinkman

Index
Elke Stevens

Design
Metahaven

Paper Inside
Munken Print 100 gr 1.5

Paper Cover
Bioset 240 gr

Printing and Binding
Bariet Ten Brink, Meppel
Reprint POD, Scanlaser, Zaandam

Publisher
Valiz, Amsterdam, 2019/POD, 2024
www.valiz.nl

ISBN 978-94-92095-46-6

This publication was made possible through the generous support of:

KONE FOUNDATION

ACADEMY OF FINE ARTS
UNIARTS HELSINKI

SAASTAMOISEN SÄÄTIÖ

frame contemporary art finland

ARIA
Antwerp Research Institute for the Arts
University of Antwerp

iaspis

Distribution:
USA/Canada/Latin America: D.A.P., www.artbook.com
GB/IE: Anagram Books, www.anagrambooks.com
NL/BE/LU: Centraal Boekhuis, www.cb.nl
Europe/Asia: Idea Books, www.ideabooks.nl
Australia: Perimeter Books, www.perimeterdistribution.com

ISBN 978-94-92095-46-6

Printed and bound in the Netherlands

Antennae

Antennae Series

Antennae N° 1
The Fall of the Studio
Artists at Work
edited by Wouter Davidts & Kim Paice
Amsterdam: Valiz, 2009
(2nd ed.: 2010),
ISBN 978-90-78088-29-5

Antennae N° 2
Take Place
Photography and Place from Multiple Perspectives
edited by Helen Westgeest
Amsterdam: Valiz, 2009,
ISBN 978-90-78088-35-6

Antennae N° 3
The Murmuring of the Artistic Multitude
Global Art, Memory and Post-Fordism
Pascal Gielen (author)
Arts *in* Society
Amsterdam: Valiz, 2009
(2nd ed.: 2011),
ISBN 978-90-78088-34-9

Antennae N° 4
Locating the Producers
Durational Approaches to Public Art
edited by Paul O'Neill & Claire Doherty
Amsterdam: Valiz, 2011, ISBN 978-90-78088-51-6

Antennae N° 5
Community Art
The Politics of Trespassing
edited by Paul De Bruyne & Pascal Gielen
Arts *in* Society
Amsterdam: Valiz, 2011 (2nd ed.: 2013),
ISBN 978-90-78088-50-9

Antennae N° 6
See it Again, Say it Again
The Artist as Researcher
edited by Janneke Wesseling
Amsterdam: Valiz, 2011, ISBN 978-90-78088-53-0

Antennae N° 7
Teaching Art in the Neoliberal Realm
Realism versus Cynicism
edited by Pascal Gielen & Paul De Bruyne
Arts *in* Society
Amsterdam: Valiz, 2012
(2nd ed.: 2013),
ISBN 978-90-78088-57-8

Antennae N° 8
Institutional Attitudes
Instituting Art in a Flat World
edited by Pascal Gielen
Arts *in* Society
Amsterdam: Valiz, 2013, ISBN 978-90-78088-68-4

Antennae N° 9
Dread
The Dizziness of Freedom
edited by Juha van 't Zelfde
Amsterdam: Valiz, 2013, ISBN 978-90-78088-81-3

Antennae N° 10
Participation Is Risky
Approaches to Joint Creative Processes
edited by Liesbeth Huybrechts
Amsterdam: Valiz, 2014, ISBN 978-90-78088-77-6

Antennae N° 11
The Ethics of Art
Ecological Turns in the Performing Arts
edited by Guy Cools & Pascal Gielen
Arts *in* Society
Amsterdam: Valiz, 2014, ISBN 978-90-78088-87-5

Antennae N° 12
Alternative Mainstream
Making Choices in Pop Music
Gert Keunen (author)
Arts *in* Society
Amsterdam: Valiz, 2014,
ISBN 978-90-78088-95-0

Antennae N° 13
The Murmuring of the Artistic
Global Art, Politics and Post-Fordism
Pascal Gielen (author)
Completely revised and enlarged edition of Antennae N° 3
Arts *in* Society
Amsterdam: Valiz, 2015,
ISBN 978-94-92095-04-6

Antennae N° 14
Aesthetic Justice
Intersecting Artistic and Moral Perspectives
edited by Pascal Gielen &
Niels Van Tomme
Arts *in* Society
Amsterdam: Valiz, 2015,
ISBN 978-90-78088-86-8

Antennae N° 15
No Culture, No Europe
On the Foundation of Politics
edited by Pascal Gielen
Arts *in* Society
Amsterdam: Valiz, 2015,
ISBN 978-94-92095-03-9

Antennae N° 16
Arts Education Beyond Art
Teaching Art in Times of Change
edited by Barend van Heusden &
Pascal Gielen
Arts *in* Society
Amsterdam: Valiz, 2015,
ISBN 978-90-78088-85-1

Antennae N° 17
Mobile Autonomy
Exercises in Artists' Self-Organization
edited by Nico Dockx & Pascal
Gielen
Arts *in* Society
Amsterdam: Valiz, 2015,
ISBN 978-94-92095-10-7

Antennae N° 18
Moving Together
Theorizing and Making
Contemporary Dance
Rudi Laermans (author)
Arts *in* Society
Amsterdam: Valiz, 2015,
ISBN 978-90-78088-52-3

Antennae N° 19
Spaces for Criticism
Shifts in Contemporary Art Discourses
edited by Thijs Lijster, Suzana
Milevska, Pascal Gielen,
Ruth Sonderegger
Arts *in* Society
Amsterdam: Valiz, 2015,
ISBN 978-90-78088-75-2

Antennae N° 20
Interrupting the City
Artistic Constitutions of the Public Sphere
edited by Sander Bax, Pascal Gielen
& Bram Ieven
Arts *in* Society
Amsterdam: Valiz, 2015,
ISBN 978-94-92095-02-2

Antennae N° 21
In-between Dance Cultures
On the Migratory Artistic Identity of
Sidi Larbi Cherkaoui and Akram Khan
Guy Cools (author)
Arts *in* Society
Amsterdam: Valiz, 2015,
ISBN 978-94-92095-11-4

Antennae N° 22
Imaginative Bodies
Dialogues in Performance Practices
Guy Cools (author)
Arts *in* Society
Amsterdam: Valiz, 2016,
ISBN 978-94-92095-20-6

Antennae N° 23
The Practice of Dramaturgy
Working on Actions in Performance
edited by Konstantina Georgelou,
Efrosini Protopapa,
Danae Theodoridou
Arts *in* Society
Amsterdam: Valiz, 2017,
ISBN: 978-94-92095-18-3

Antennae N° 24
The Art of Civil Action
Political Space and Cultural Dissent
edited by Philipp Dietachmair,
Pascal Gielen
Arts *in* Society
Amsterdam: Valiz, 2017,
ISBN: 978-94-92095-39-8

Antennae N° 25
Commonism
A New Aesthetics of the Real
Nico Dockx & Pascal Gielen
Arts *in* Society
Amsterdam: Valiz, 2018,
ISBN 978-94-92095-47-3

Antennae N° 26
The Future of the New
Artistic Innovation in Times
of Social Acceleration
Thijs Lijster (ed.)
Arts *in* Society
Amsterdam: Valiz, 2018,
ISBN 978-94-92095-53-9